*The Delusion of Disbelief*

# THE DE

# DIS

# LUSION
## OF
# BELIEF

## DAVID AIKMAN

SALT**RIVER**®

AN IMPRINT OF
Tyndale House Publishers, Inc., Carol Stream, Illinois

This book is dedicated to my cherished, wonderful friend, who was loyal and helpful at a great personal cost.

Visit Tyndale's exciting Web site at www.tyndale.com

*SaltRiver* and the SaltRiver logo are registered trademarks of Tyndale Hosue Publishers, Inc.

*The Delusion of Disbelief: Why the New Atheism Is a Threat to Your Life, Liberty, and Pursuit of Happiness*

Designed by Erik M. Peterson

Published in association with the literary agency of Eames Literary Services, 4170 Hillsboro Rd., Suite 251, Nashville, TN 37215.

Unless otherwise indicated, all Scripture quotations are taken from the Holy Bible, New International Version®. NIV®. Copyright © 1973, 1978, 1984 by International Bible Society. Used by permission of Zondervan. All rights reserved.

Scripture quotations marked RSV are taken from the *Holy Bible*, Revised Standard Version, copyright © 1946, 1952, 1971 by the Division of Christian Education of the National Council of the Churches of Christ in the United States of America, and are used by permission. All rights reserved.

**Library of Congress Cataloging-in-Publication Data**

Aikman, David, date.
　　The delusion of disbelief : why the new atheism is a threat to your life, liberty, and pursuit of happiness / David Aikman.
　　　　p. cm.
　　Includes bibliographical references and index.
　　ISBN-13: 978-1-4143-1708-3 (hc)
　　ISBN-10: 1-4143-1708-5 (hc)
　　1. Atheism.　I. Title.
　　BL2747.3.A35 2008
　　211′.8—dc22
　　　　　　　　　　　　　　　　　　　　　　　　　　　　　　　2007044539

Printed in the United States of America

14　13　12　11　10　09　08
　7　　6　　5　　4　　3　　2　　1

# CONTENTS

# Chapter One

# THE
# FOUR HORSEMEN

*"Ours is the first attempt in recorded history to build
a culture upon the premise that God is dead."*
— Princeton theologian Paul Ramsey, in 1966

A great assault upon faith was launched in 2006 against unsuspecting Americans who attend church, go to synagogue, worship in mosques, pray in temples, or otherwise live lives in which religion plays an important role. In just over a half year, three books by atheists hit the bookstores. Each of these books in various ways attacks all religious belief in general and Christianity in particular. *Letter to a Christian Nation*, written by a doctoral candidate in neuroscience, Sam Harris, came out on September 19, just a day after the publication of *The God Delusion* by Richard Dawkins, a noted British ethologist, evolutionary biologist, and Oxford University professor. The third book, *Breaking the Spell: Religion as a Natural Phenomenon*, by Daniel Dennett, a Tufts University philosophy professor, was released earlier, in February 2006.

All were best sellers and by mid-2007, the print run for *Breaking the Spell* had reached 64,000. *The God Delusion* was at 500,000, and *Letter to a Christian Nation* was at 185,000. Both the Harris and the Dawkins books were also on *Publishers Weekly*'s 2006 best seller list.

Meanwhile, as Americans of faith were still digesting this burst of atheistic book production, one of the most talented writers and journalists in America, Englishman (and newly naturalized U.S. citizen) Christopher Hitchens, was about to uncoil his own sling. *God Is Not Great: How Religion Poisons Everything* was published on May 1, 2007. It was certainly a brisk seller; when I tried to buy a copy at the Borders bookstore on L Street in Washington D.C. less than two weeks later, I was told that it was sold out and that the store was scrambling to get more. In just a month's time, the book had debuted at the No. 1 slot on the *New York Times* best sellers list with sales of more than 58,000. By the third week of June, just seven weeks after *God Is Not Great*'s release, 296,000 copies were in print, bringing the total copies in print of all four atheist titles to more than one million.

Harris, Dawkins, Dennett, and Hitchens—the names resonate like stately Anglo-Saxon partners of a Virginia law firm[1] —descended upon the faithful like, well, the Four Horsemen of the Apocalypse. (For those who are unfamiliar with the Bible, or even with the biblically-derived imagery of Western art and literature, the Four Horsemen of the Apocalypse appear in the sixth chapter of the New Testament book of Revelation and have traditionally been regarded as corresponding to Pestilence, Famine, War, and Death.) Indeed, these four atheist writers have already been called the Four Horsemen in a review that appeared in *The Chronicle of Higher Education*, a Washington D.C.–based weekly newspaper for American college and university faculty.[2]

Richard Dawkins uses the less glowering literary reference "The Four Musketeers" on his own Web site (http://richard dawkins.net) in welcoming Christopher Hitchens to the gang of faithslayers. A far less flattering nickname would be "The Gang of Four," a term that was disseminated with great effect by leaders in Communist China to denigrate four ultra-leftist politicians in a Beijing coup d'état after the death of Chairman Mao Tse-tung in 1976.[3] But that might be unfair. It is enough to say that Dawkins and his allies have been referred to as "the new Godless," "the New Atheists," and "fundamentalist atheists," among other sobriquets.

The publishing phenomenon that these authors triggered quickly spilled over into other forums all over the country, and even beyond American shores. National radio and television news talk shows pitted the authors in debates against evangelical Christians. The Internet quickly bristled with angry diatribes from both camps. Major secular and Christian magazines invited the authors and Christian leaders to defend their views. Book reviews cropped up in a surprising array of publications—print and online, American and European, religious and secular, scientific and atheistic, general news and scholarly. Journalists from Germany to Australia trumpeted the news that America was experiencing a new rise of atheism. Even China's official national television network, CCTV, and a Chinese-language Christian magazine reported on the phenomenon, and some Christians on mainland China started circulating essays attacking the New Atheists.

Groups across the United States booked the authors to speak at venues ranging from a Unitarian church to the New York Public Library, as well as any number of college campuses. New videos showing one or another of the authors or some parody of them cropped up on YouTube just about every week. Dawkins wrote of one grueling day in Toronto when he was booked for "five television interviews and one radio, all in one day beginning before breakfast."[4] The phenomenon was so widespread that it even made it into the pages of the Sunday "funnies." That's not a place where discussions of this sort are normally found, but on June 17, the "Opus" strip commented on the "surprising trend" of atheist best-selling books.[5] Indeed, this has been a surprising trend, but it clearly indicates that the coterie of Dawkins, Dennett, Harris, & Hitchens has touched a nerve. "This is atheism's moment," exulted one publishing house CEO.[6]

It is true that atheists are enjoying a rare prominence in American society, where their numbers have always been small. In March 2007, *Newsweek* magazine reported the results of a poll in which people were asked, "Are you an atheist?" A mere 3 percent of respondents said they were atheists, while 96 percent said they were not and 1 percent answered "don't know."[7] (Hitchens has claimed there may be as many as 15 million atheists in the United States, which would be closer to

6 percent of the population.) Only 29 percent in the *Newsweek* poll said they would vote for an atheist for president, down from 37 percent in 2006 and 49 percent in 1996. In other polls, atheists have received the highest disapproval rating of all identifiable social groups as possible future spouses of one's children: 48 percent, as opposed to 34 percent for Muslims and 27 percent for African Americans.[8]

Atheists were also considered "least likely" to share the average American's "vision" of America.[9] In April 2006, *American Sociological Review* reported on a study that found it is still socially acceptable, in the United States at least, to say you are intolerant of atheists.[10] In *The God Delusion*, Dawkins cites his own figures illustrating the isolation of atheists in America. He refers to a 1999 Gallup poll that asked Americans whether they would vote for an otherwise well-qualified person who was:

A woman—95 percent said they would.
A Roman Catholic—94 percent
A Jew—92 percent
An African American—92 percent
A Mormon—79 percent
A homosexual—79 percent
An atheist—49 percent

The last statistic in this list seems especially to have riled Dawkins. In *The God Delusion*, he speaks often of a need for "consciousness-raising" among atheists in America, and the need for atheists to "come out," much as homosexuals have been doing in ever-larger numbers in recent decades. He writes almost wistfully, "My dream is that this book may help people to come out."[11] For those who may need some friendly encouragement to do so, Dawkins provides in his book a helpful five-page appendix entitled "A partial list of friendly addresses, for individuals needing support in escaping from religion."[12] His Web site has a social-networking section that serves as a platform for putting atheists from around the world in touch with each other.

In 2003, Dawkins and Dennett wrote a series of editorials trying to popularize a new nomenclature for atheists: "the brights." Ostensibly, this was to provide atheists with their own version of "gay pride" and a sort of umbrella of respectability to protect atheists from the real or imagined prejudice of many Americans. Today, there is a brights Web site, www.the-brights.net. Not surprisingly though, the term *brights* has provoked a backlash from those offended by the pretentiousness of the term, and not only among nonatheists. On National Public Radio, a commentator discussing the notion of "brights" drily observed, "The rest of us would be the 'Dims,' I suppose . . . [t]hey might as well have chosen the word 'The Smugs' or 'The Smarty-Pants.'"[13] Dawkins, moreover, has found robust disagreement with the notion of "brights" in one of his fellow Four Musketeers. Christopher Hitchens disdainfully refers to the term as both a "cringe-making proposal" and conceited, because it implies that atheists are inherently brighter people than benighted people of faith.[14]

In a report on the new atheism, the *Chicago Sun-Times* agreed that it was accurate to call its proponents "Fundamentalist atheists" because they are basing their movement on "a piece of dogma that can't be challenged without enraging them and [have] clung to the belief that contemporary American society doesn't permit the criticism of religion." The author points out the irony of this view, saying, "They hold this belief so strongly that they've written several best-selling books about it. The fact that this might be a contradiction doesn't seem to have occurred to them."[15]

If the polls cited above and Dawkins's assertion of American intolerance of atheists are accurate, then we "dims" do indeed need to behave better. It is surely the mark of any civilized society that philosophical and political adversaries conduct discourse with respect and courtesy. As Catholic theologian and former U.S. ambassador Michael Novak has observed, "*Civilization is constituted by reasoned conversation. Civilized humans converse with one another, argue with one another, offer evidence to one another. Barbarians club one another*" (emphasis in the original).[16] Of course, everyone knows that this principle of civilized behavior is often ignored, in the realm of politics certainly, but increasingly also in what passes for humorous conversation on TV and radio talk shows.

Curiously, in some atheistic rants about religion, the verbal content of vulgarity and obscenity seems to be exceptionally high.[17] For some reason, the discourse of atheists in Britain has been more decorous; Dawkins would almost certainly not utter an

7

obscenity on-camera in England. Perhaps the propensity for foul language in America is because atheists here enjoy "shocking" religious people.[18] Christians, however, even if they don't use obscenities with any regularity, have been just as guilty of abusive discourse with their opponents, even when those opponents are fellow believers.[19] There can be no excuse for this.

It was Sam Harris's *Letter to a Christian Nation* that initially prompted me to write this book.[20] *Letter*, as it happens, was written in response to critical letters Harris received from readers responding to his first book, *The End of Faith: Religion, Terror, and the Future of Reason.* That book, Harris has explained, was inspired by his realization after September 11, 2001, that it was religious belief that had provoked nineteen Arab hijackers to commandeer U.S. airplanes and crash them into the World Trade Center, the Pentagon, and a field in Pennsylvania. Harris thought that it was time to challenge the validity of religious faith itself. *The End of Faith* was initially rejected by several publishers because of its disparaging views on religion—particularly on Islam. When it was finally published in 2004, though, it not only sold 275,000 copies and debuted at No. 4 on the *New York Times* Best Sellers list, where it had a thirty-three-week run, it was also awarded the 2005 PEN/Martha Albrand Award for First Nonfiction.

In *Letter to a Christian Nation*, Harris writes that he received thousands of e-mails and letters from people saying that he was wrong not to believe in God. "The most hostile came from Christians," he said, adding, "The truth is that many who claim to be transformed by Christ's love are deeply, even murderously, intolerant of criticism. While we may want to ascribe this to human nature," he continued, "it is clear that such hatred draws considerable support from the Bible. How do I know this? The most disturbed of my correspondents always cite chapter and verse."[21]

Well, I am certainly not disturbed by Harris's books. Outspoken atheists have been writing and publishing since at least the middle of the eighteenth century, and their ranks have been filled with some talented and powerful intellects: Enlightenment-era French philosopher and writer Denis Diderot; eighteenth-century French-German author Paul-Henri Thiry, baron d'Holbach; nineteenth-century German philosopher Ludwig Andreas Feuerbach; "father of Communism" Karl Marx and his collaborator, Friedrich Engels; German philosopher Friedrich Nietzsche who famously declared, "God is dead"; American Freethought orator Robert G. Ingersoll; "father of psychoanalysis" Sigmund Freud; Bertrand Russell, one of the founders of analytic philosophy; and French existentialist philosopher Jean-Paul Sartre, among others.

Nor is this the first time in recent decades that God's existence and relevance have been questioned. A similar groundswell of atheistic activity culminated in a *Time* magazine cover story on April 8, 1966 (Easter Sunday, as it happens), that asked, "Is God Dead?" It turned out to be one of the newsmagazine's most controversial cover stories, and in it Princeton theologian Paul Ramsey was quoted as saying, "Ours is the first attempt in recorded history to build a culture upon the premise that God is dead."[22] With the benefit of hindsight, of course, we now know that that attempt failed. And it has to be said that this time around, none of the Four Horsemen succeeds in knocking religion out of the ring either, though cumulatively they do make some strong, and sometimes valid points against it. Their failure lies in at least one of the following: Their assertions are too wild to be taken seriously (does Hitchens *really* think that religion has done nothing good at all in the entire history of humanity?); when they stray into the terrain of biblical studies, they show an amazing unfamiliarity with it; and their view that the discoveries of science have invalidated religious truth is entirely rejected by an impressive group of reputable scientists.

Of course, in asserting the rudeness of his Christian correspondents, Harris underlines the point he first made in *The End of Faith*, which is that religion doesn't make people behave better toward each other. But Harris goes further. He also asserts that in writing *Letter*, he "set out to demolish the intellectual and moral pretensions of Christianity in its most committed forms."[23] The question therefore arises: Why this sudden upsurge of atheistic propaganda now?

A number of factors come immediately to mind, political ones being the most prominent. George W. Bush's administration has probably included more evangelical Christians serving at senior levels than that of any recent U.S. president. Cabinet secretaries, speechwriters, and White House aides who are

Christians have been outspoken about their faith. The president himself has always been forthright about his religious convictions. In fact, when candidates were asked during a presidential debate to name the philosopher they most admired, Bush answered unequivocally, Jesus—a turning point in his 2000 primary campaign.[24] Since becoming president, Bush has been careful not to speak much in public about his faith, limiting his comments to expressions of gratitude to the many Americans who say they are praying for him. Privately, he has gone to church most Sundays that he is in Washington, and he has, at different times, invited clergy with whom he is close to the White House or Camp David.

This open display of Christian belief has not, it seems, troubled the majority of Americans. In the aforementioned March 2007 *Newsweek* poll, less than one-third (32 percent) of respondents agreed that "organized religion has too much influence on American politics." Just as many (31 percent) said it had "too little," and 29 percent that it had the "right amount." This is hardly surprising considering that 82 percent of respondents in the same poll called themselves "Christian," a figure in keeping with polling results that regularly show upwards of 70 percent of Americans identifying themselves as "Christian."[25] Moreover, as The Barna Group found in its annual poll on the state of American faith in May 2007, 40 percent of Christians call themselves "born again" (which translates into 90 million Americans), and 43 percent said they attended church the previous week.[26] In the 2004 election, "born-agains" voted overwhelmingly for Bush: 62 percent, as compared with 38 percent for Kerry.

This overt American religiosity is troubling, however, to some overseas observers of the United States, many of whom work in media or academia and tend to be secular in their outlook on life and therefore are uncomprehending of the piety of Americans. This piety is also just downright irritating to some, especially British observers, who like to caricature all popular American Protestant religious leaders as modern-day Elmer Gantrys, shysters in clerical garb. In their view, religious belief should be a private affair, and the way many Americans wear it on their sleeves is unseemly.

Another factor is uniting atheists on both sides of the Atlantic as well. It is the progress that lobbyists for "intelligent design" have made in the American educational system in their campaign to have Darwinism treated as an as-yet-unproven theory and not taught as scientific fact. Many scholars of Darwinian evolution have insisted that Darwinism inevitably confirms atheism. Richard Dawkins is one of them, and his dogmatism in this vein has aroused bitter criticism among other evolutionary scientists. Michael Ruse, a prominent Darwinian philosopher and agnostic, is one who has been deeply irritated by Dawkins's view. "Dawkins and Dennett are really dangerous," he complains, "both at a moral and a legal level." Ruse argues that Darwinism is not inherently atheistic, and to claim that it is gives advocates of intelligent design a legal basis for their cause. After all, if they can show that Darwinism is a concept synonymous with atheism, then to teach Darwinism in American public schools is to teach atheism, and that would violate the nonestablishment clause of the First Amendment to the U.S. Constitution prohibiting a state-run church.[27] "It gives the creationists a legal case. Dawkins and Dennett are handing these people a major tool," Ruse argues.[28]

When these cultural and scientific views are coupled with the deep political unpopularity of the Bush administration because of the Iraq War, the combination is combustible. It has been easy to conflate the widespread dissatisfaction over the Iraq War with evangelical Christianity in general, especially since the Bush administration has openly appealed to conservative Christians for political support and because most observers have asserted that conservative Christians are the strongest supporters of Bush's Iraq War policy.[29] Many overseas observers have seized upon Bush's religious faith to explain his decision to launch the Iraq War—a view in line with the premise promoted by the atheists' books that, contrary to conventional wisdom, religion is not a force for good.

Apart from these political reasons, though, there is the very real possibility of a cultural backlash against evangelical conservatives in general in the United States. As Bush's two terms wind down, there are clearly segments of American society that have tired of the religious content of the public discourse of recent years. After six years of an administration that promoted "faith-based" initiatives for solving social problems—trying to undo the "progressive" legislation of the Clinton years

(1993–2001) on gay rights and abortion issues—and after six years of sometimes triumphalistic rhetoric by Christian conservatives, some sort of reaction was all but inevitable.

Although Americans for the most part have all along favorably viewed the expression of religious belief in the public domain, it is also the case that Americans don't like exaggerated or extreme examples of that expression. As Hitchens's publisher Jonathan Karp put it: "It's a manifestation of the anger that people are feeling toward piety in the culture, fears about Islamic extremism and frustration with the way religion is continuously injected into our political life."[30] Fair play and equal opportunity are treasured American principles, and it may simply be that after two terms of conservatives and people of faith holding leadership positions in Washington, Americans think it is time for the other side to have a say about things.

If that is true of Americans, it is doubly true of British and other European observers. British observers in particular see broader historical analogies. In *God's Funeral*, British author A. N. Wilson recounts the way many leading nineteenth-century British intellectuals abandoned belief in God: historian Thomas Carlyle, philosopher John Stuart Mill, novelist George Eliot, literary critic Matthew Arnold, art critic John Ruskin, poet Algernon Swinburne. If there is one generalization that can be made about Victorian atheism, it is this: Intellectuals embraced atheism as much out of moral revulsion at what they considered Christianity's failure to address contemporary social ills such as child abuse, troubled marriages, and inadequate rights for women as in response to Charles Darwin's discoveries about evolution or the Communist creeds of Karl Marx.

Wilson, himself a Christian-turned-atheist, makes an interesting point, however. The nineteenth century may have noted God's funeral (the book title is taken from a poem by English poet Thomas Hardy), but, Wilson says, "One of the most extraordinary things about the twentieth century has been the palpable and visible strength of the Christian thing, the Christian idea."[31] Wilson cites such outstanding, and indeed heroic, figures as French philosopher Simone Weil, German theologian Dietrich Bonhoeffer, Russian philosopher Nikolay Berdyayev, and French priest and philosopher Pierre Teilhard de Chardin—heroic because they each used faith to resist barbarous totalitarianism.

Wilson might have included on that list Aleksandr Solzhenitsyn, the Russian Nobel Prize laureate in literature whose writings were instrumental in undermining the entire existence of the Soviet Union, because their truth-telling accounts of Stalin's gulag destroyed the Soviet experiment's last pretension to moral legitimacy.[32] Wilson also notes the role of Dr. Martin Luther King Jr. in standing up to institutional racism in the United States, and of Anglican clergyman Trevor Huddleston in accomplishing the same against apartheid in South Africa.

As Wilson is forced to admit in the book's closing sentences, though he remains unpersuaded by Christianity or any other form of theism, "These world-changing men and women decided to ignore the death of God in the nineteenth century. They spoke in the name of a God who was First and Last. They put their trust in One who said, 'I was dead, and see, I am alive for evermore.'"[33] For an atheist, that's powerfully and truthfully spoken. To put a twist on one of the most famous sayings of Mark Twain, who incidentally was not a believer in God, "The reports of God's death are greatly exaggerated."[34]

# Chapter Two

# THE
# ATTACK
## OF THE
# FOUR HORSEMEN

*"The argument with faith is the foundation and origin of all
arguments, because it is the beginning—but not the end—of all
arguments about philosophy, science, history, and human nature."*
— Christopher Hitchens, *God Is Not Great*

The Four Horsemen are not a coordinated or coherent
group, though by adopting the nickname the "Four
Musketeers" on his Web site, Oxford professor Richard
Dawkins tries to convey the image of a cheerful band of adven-
turers. Indeed, their books are full of mutual backslapping and
effusive compliments for each other, as though they are grizzled
fellow veterans sharing a joke after fighting the forces of darkness and superstition. Dawkins, the elder brother of the four,
refers to Daniel Dennett (just plain "Dan" to his intimates) as
"my friend the philosopher"[1] or "that scientifically savvy philosopher."[2] He quotes Sam Harris at paragraph-length, with

such approving commentary as "Sam Harris is magnificently scathing"[3] or "Sam Harris, as so often, hits the bullseye."[4] As for Christopher Hitchens, Dawkins joins the gang of Mother Teresa bashers by recommending Hitchens's hatchet job on the Calcutta nun, the book *The Missionary Position: Mother Teresa in Theory and Practice*.[5] Dennett is scarcely less effusive toward Dawkins: "As Richard Dawkins succinctly puts it" (in talking about the earth-god Gaia)[6] or "Dawkins reminds me of my grandfather" (who was so farsighted in pointing out the dangers of secondhand smoke long before its dangers were widely accepted).[7] Dennett calls Harris's *The End of Faith* "a brave book."[8] Only Hitchens, his dyspeptic tongue reluctant to join the Four Musketeers' general good cheer, growls with annoyance, as noted in the previous chapter, at Dawkins and Dennett for championing the term *brights* to refer to atheists. Nonetheless, he is no less unwavering than the others in his atheistic convictions, and indeed is the most voluble promoter of them all.

The four authors, though, vary in their reasons for atheism as well as in their approach, their tone, and even their arguments, sometimes actually contradicting each other. Of course, just as religious believers have differing interpretations and different understandings of the same religion, so it is not surprising that atheists would differ from each other about their beliefs. The differences among the Four Horsemen in some ways reflect their backgrounds and life experiences.

Senior horseman Richard Dawkins is the oldest and academically best established of the group. Born in Kenya in 1941, he graduated with a degree in zoology from Oxford's Balliol College in 1962. He holds two doctorates from Oxford, the first of which he earned in 1966. After two years of teaching at the University of California, Berkeley, Dawkins returned to Oxford in 1970 as a lecturer. In 1995, he became the first occupant of the Charles Simonyi Professorship for the Public Understanding of Science at Oxford University, a post he still holds. Simonyi, a billionaire computer software executive who headed Microsoft's application software group for two decades, insisted from the outset that Dawkins be the first occupant of the endowed chair.

Dawkins had come to fame in 1976 with the publication of *The Selfish Gene*, an elegantly written book that describes in highly readable, popular language the central role of genes in Darwinian evolution. In the course of the next few years, as his reputation as a skillful literary popularizer of science grew, so did his fame as a militant atheist. In 1996, Charles Simonyi described him as "Darwin's Rottweiler," a reference to Dawkins's increasingly polemical approach toward religious belief in the context of the alleged scientific validity of evolution. Dawkins has become so identified with an assault upon religion that he has also been described as "the nearest thing to a professional atheist since Bertrand Russell,"[9] one of the most prominent atheists of the twentieth century. A *New Yorker* profile called him "Britain's village atheist."[10]

The second of the Four Horsemen, Daniel Dennett, has

been a friend and ally of Dawkins since reading and being impressed by *The Selfish Gene*. Just a year younger than Dawkins, Dennett has equally impressive academic credentials and has been described as the "less argumentative and more analytical" of the two.[11] He is the Austin B. Fletcher Professor of Philosophy and the codirector of the Center for Cognitive Studies at Tufts University, as well as the author of more than a dozen books. Like Dawkins, Dennett's childhood was lived overseas—in his case, Beirut. After earning a bachelor's degree in philosophy at Harvard University, he went to Oxford and studied the philosophy of ordinary language under the late and famous Professor Gilbert Ryle, earning a doctorate in 1965. He claims to have introduced the Frisbee to Britain by deploying one on Worcester College gardens. I have to admit, as an undergraduate member of the college at that time, I never saw it happen.

After Oxford, Dennett went on to become a distinguished philosopher working in the area of philosophy of mind and consciousness, with strong interests in the philosophy of science and the philosophy of biology. The recipient of numerous awards and a man of broad talents and interests (he was so accomplished both as a sculptor and a pianist that he considered pursuing sculpting or jazz music professionally), he developed a strong interest in Darwinism and became fascinated by the ways the theory of evolution explained developments of the mind and consciousness. In 2003, he started advocating that atheists be called "brights," taking the lead and "coming out" as a "bright" at a conference in Seattle and then writing about the experience in *The New York Times*.[12]

The third of the Four Horsemen in age (though his book *God Is Not Great* was the fourth to hit the bookstores) is yet another Oxonian, that is, a graduate of Oxford University. Christopher Hitchens, an Englishman like Dawkins, was born in Portsmouth, England, in 1949, and also like Dawkins, graduated from Oxford's Balliol College, though with a degree in philosophy, politics, and economics (popularly known as "PPE"). Hitchens, however, was no great scholar, and having graduated with an undistinguished "third class" degree,[13] he did not enter academic life as Dawkins and Dennett had, but went into journalism, making a name for himself as a feisty writer for Britain's left-of-center weekly, *The New Statesman*. At Oxford and in the years immediately after his 1970 graduation, Hitchens had been a Marxist and a Trotskyist, and his first journalistic work after graduating was for the Trotskyite magazine *International Socialism*.

Hitchens immigrated to the United States in 1981 and began writing the next year for *The Nation*, a left-wing magazine that in the 1980s was fiercely opposed to President Reagan and often devoted space to the Soviet viewpoint in the Cold War. While at *The Nation*, Hitchens wrote a number of books on quite varied topics: *The Missionary Position*, about Mother Teresa, in 1995; *No One Left to Lie To: Values of the Worst Family*, about President Clinton, in 1999; and *The Trial of Henry Kissinger*, in 2001.[14] In all these books, Hitchens showed both brilliance and a streak of malice. He does not suffer fools gladly, is a verbally deft debater, and on TV talk shows in recent years has trashed the audience with four-letter words. The verbal slash-and-burn tactics have characterized both his TV appearances and his writing, whether that be his books or his columns in *Vanity Fair*, where he has been a contributing editor since 2001.

It is hard to tell whether Hitchens is relentlessly provocative and uncharitable (for example, just days after Rev. Jerry Falwell died in May 2007, Hitchens called him "a toad" and claimed Falwell didn't even believe the things he preached) for the perverse pleasure of annoying people or because he is someone of such high moral indignation that it cannot be tempered by the normal constraints of civility. Nathan Katz, a professor of religious studies at Florida International University, described Hitchens at an appearance in Miami opposite an orthodox Jew and a Buddhist nun as "utterly abusive" and said the event "had the intellectual level of the Jerry Springer Show."[15]

In fact, though, Hitchens does have a rightful claim to the moral high ground—assuming there is an understanding of the term *moral* that religious people and secularists can agree on—in several important areas of national and international concern. After Iran's Ayatollah Khomeini issued his infamous death fatwa against Hitchens's longtime friend British novelist Salman Rushdie for writing the novel *The Satanic Verses*, Hitchens courageously opened his apartment in Washington, D.C., to Rushdie as a hiding place, incurring the predictable shower of Islamist insults and threats. He has also deeply offended his former friends and colleagues of the left by strongly supporting the U.S. invasion of Iraq and the toppling of Saddam Hussein, as well as by standing by Paul Wolfowitz in 2007 when Wolfowitz was under intense pressure to resign from the presidency of the World Bank. In 2002, after increasingly acrimonious debates in print with one of America's principal leftist intellectuals, Noam Chomsky, over the nature of the threat of radical Islam, Hitchens resigned from *The Nation*, where he had been a columnist for ten years.

Even more impressively, Hitchens has cast a gimlet eye upon a particularly disturbing phenomenon: the emergence of a viciously antidemocratic alliance of the left—in Europe and the United States—with apologists and even advocates of murderous Islamic radicalism. The left, while praiseworthy over the decades for opposing racism, campaigning for civil rights for minorities (and not just for racial minorities), and pointing to many of the cruelties of capitalism, has had a curious tendency to be entirely myopic toward much greater dangers to itself and to civilized life in general than capitalist liberal democracy ever has been.

When he debated Chris Hedges, a former *New York Times* reporter who thinks American Christian conservatives are as dangerous to American democracy as Mussolini's fascists were, Hitchens forthrightly attacked Islamist terrorism's use of suicide bombing, triggering loud booing by a large Muslim contingent in the audience at the May 2007 Berkeley, California, event. He defended American soldiers fighting in Iraq, applauding them for "creating space for secularism to emerge," and excoriated what he called "the evil nonsense taught by Hedges and friends of his, who say the suicide bombers in Palestine are driven to it by despair." Pointing toward Hedges at the conclusion of his remarks, Hitchens said, "A perfect picture has been given to you of the cretinous relationship between sloppy moral relativism, half-baked religious absolutism, and the journalism that lies in between."[16] When the moderator turned to Hedges to see if he would respond, he waved his hand in refusal.

In debates, Hitchens is tart, extremely quick-witted, and merciless to his opponents, regardless of their political or religious (or nonreligious) perspective. But he gets as good as he gives. In a broadly publicized public dispute in Washington D.C. with British Respect Party MP George Galloway, who was both a fawning admirer of Saddam Hussein and a vituperative critic of President George W. Bush, Galloway famously described Hitchens as "a drink-sodden former Trotskyist popinjay." The folkloric nature of the confrontation has even inspired a new Web site with a reference to Galloway's insult at http://drinksoakedtrotsforwar.com. Hitchens has freely confessed that he likes to drink alcohol copiously; he denies doing so in excess.

The youngest of the Four Horsemen is another American, and it was his book *The End of Faith: Religion, Terror, and the Future of Reason*[17] that helped launch this new atheist upsurge in the first place. A pleasant-mannered young man with impeccable West Coast credentials, Sam Harris in many respects has had a more mysterious career than any of the others. Born to a Jewish mother and a Quaker father in 1967 (Hitchens is also Jewish through his mother), he holds a Stanford University degree in philosophy. In 1986, he and a friend experimented with the hallucinogenic drug MDMA, better known by its street name, "ecstasy." Harris experienced some kind of mind-altering epiphany and decided to drop out of college, apparently to write a novel. He spent the next eleven years traveling through India and Nepal and experimenting with meditation techniques at retreat centers in Marin County, California, and Massachusetts, where he would meditate for up to eighteen hours at a time. He then returned to Stanford and completed his degree.

Harris has said that his interest in demolishing religious belief surfaced after the September 11 terror attacks, when he came to the conclusion that religion in the generic sense was what had prompted the nineteen Muslim Arabs to crash four airliners in New York, Washington, and Pennsylvania, killing close to 3,500 people. His first book, *The End of Faith*, was a surprise best seller that led to his second, *Letter to a Christian Nation*, a much shorter book—more of an essay in book form—that was also a best seller. The success of *Letter* was helped no doubt by the two hundred thousand dollars his publisher, Knopf, spent on an ad campaign "aimed at both preaching to the converted and trying to rile the opposition," according to the *Wall Street Journal*. A Knopf spokesman told the newspaper, "We're trying to get this book into the hands of as many conservative Christians as possible. They have a vested interest in hearing Mr. Harris's arguments because he's attacking the very foundation of their belief system."[18]

Little is known of Harris's current personal life; he discloses few personal details because of security concerns stemming from what he has described as "some reasonably scary e-mails"[19] and will not even reveal at which university he is currently pursuing a graduate degree in neuroscience (although news reports as recently as 2005 said he was a doctoral candidate at UCLA). He has, however, frequently conducted TV and other public debates with critics of his anti-God position.

Harris has been joined on the TV, radio, and lecture circuit by Dawkins and Hitchens. Dennett has been almost reclusive by comparison, but his low profile may be due to health issues (he had a nine-hour heart operation in November 2006, after which he wrote with relief that his brush with death had not triggered a conversion from atheism, as has been known to have happened to some other famous atheists[20]). Dawkins wrote and produced a two-part documentary for Britain's Channel Four network called *The Root of All Evil.* The provocative program selected easy targets (fundamentalist believers in six-day creation, orthodox Jewish biblical literalists) and let them have their say on camera, but drastically cut the footage of highly intelligent critics such as Alister McGrath, the Oxford theologian who has debated Dawkins and written books critical of his worldview. Hitchens has waded through a thicket of TV talkshow appearances to promote his book, intimidating interviewers with his verbal pyrotechnics and expatiating volubly on the wickedness of religion.[21] But he has been by far the most intelligent and interesting debater on the topic, participating not only in highly politicized confrontations (for example, with Chris Hedges, as noted above) but also in thoughtful, detailed debates on aspects of the Christian Gospels on the radio talk show of conservative Los Angeles broadcaster Hugh Hewitt.[22]

The Four Horsemen, the Four Musketeers, the Gang of Four—what seems to be the objective of their combined assault on religious belief? To judge from the authors' own words, it is nothing less than to convert believers into atheists and to destroy any rational basis on which religious faith rests. Dawkins ambles into his book's preface with comments about the need for "consciousness-raising" among atheists, to fill them with pride because, he says, in general, they are a despised and neglected group, especially in the United States. But consciousness-raising is only his initial objective. "If this book works as I intend," he declares, "religious readers who open it will be atheists when they put it down." He admits that this notion might be "presumptuous optimism" because "of course, dyed-in-the-wool faith-heads are immune to argument, their resistance built up over years of childhood indoctrination using methods that took centuries to mature (whether by evolution or design)."[23] Dawkins adds, generously, that he believes there are still people out there "whose childhood indoctrination was not too insidious, or for other reasons didn't 'take,' or whose native intelligence is strong enough to overcome it."[24]

This kind of sneering, condescending tone pervades

Dawkins's writing in the "full monte" stage of his developed atheism. It helps explain why Simonyi's "rottweiler" label for him is far more accurate than something more benign like "Darwin's attorney" or "Darwin's good friend." Dawkins has received appreciative letters from people who were formerly what he derisively calls "faith-heads" who have abandoned their delusions and come over to the side of the brights, the pleasant green pastures where clear-eyed, brave, bold, and supremely brainy atheists graze contentedly. But just as it is doubtful whether many atheists would be converted by the preaching of arrogant and condescending Christians, so the consistently surprising ignorance Dawkins displays toward the entire Christian experience wouldn't persuade most Christians of the virtues of atheism. Toward the end of the preface, Dawkins says that he won't go "out of [his] way to offend" people who are sympathetic to religion. If *The God Delusion* is an example of Dawkins behaving well, one wonders what he is like when he really takes his gloves off.

Dennett is not as pugnacious as Dawkins, and throughout *Breaking the Spell* he preserves the tone of an affable family philosopher discoursing on a difficult subject at the end of a Thanksgiving meal. Early on in the book, however, after explaining what he believes to be an urgent need to demystify religion and to account for all of its manifestations on rational, empirical grounds, Dennett acknowledges that some of his readers "will be profoundly distrustful" of the approach he is taking. "They will see me as just another liberal professor trying to cajole them out of their convictions," he adds, "and they are dead right about that—that's what I am, and that's exactly what I'm trying to do." After admitting that he has a philosophical mugging in mind, he nevertheless expresses the hope that his readers will approach the book with an open mind.[25] Elsewhere, his irritation at religion seems to get the better of him, and he expresses doubt that readers who are people of faith will have the courage even to finish the book.[26]

A strange, almost wistful pessimism about the probable failure of atheism to persuade religionists that it is true also hovers around *God Is Not Great* by Christopher Hitchens. The book has offended at least one reviewer because of inaccuracies about Jewish customs. Though expressing general admiration for Hitchens, the reviewer, author, and religious scholar Michael Oppenheimer described *God Is Not Great* as "an intellectually shoddy and factually inaccurate rush-job."[27] Hitchens, indeed, is almost slapdash when he has no patience for a topic, a trait that suggests an intellectual laziness rooted both in contempt for people who disagree with him and an arrogance about the presumed intellectual superiority of atheism. In the very first chapter, on page five, he writes, "Our belief is not a belief. Our principles are not a faith."[28] Then, on the very next page, he writes, "We believe with certainty that an ethical life can be lived without religion."[29] Huh? Hitchens is not only inconsistent in his dogmatic definitions of what atheism is or is not, he is relentlessly combative, which raises the question of whether an atheist can debate people of faith without deliberately setting out to antagonize or obliterate them. Hitchens is so indifferent as to whether he offends people that he routinely picks up negative generalizations about religion and heedlessly tosses them over his shoulder like a coarse and slovenly dinner guest.

Hitchens nevertheless makes a profound point early on in his book, which in thoughtful moments is by turns ornery and very funny (for instance, he refers to the story of an astrologer writing for a London tabloid who was fired "by means of a letter from his editor which began, 'As you will no doubt have foreseen'"). The profound point Hitchens makes is this: "The argument with faith is the foundation and origin of all arguments, because it is the beginning—but not the end—of all arguments about philosophy, science, history, and human nature." Hitchens, a former Marxist, may unconsciously be taking up a Marxist quote that he surely knows well: "The criticism of religion is the prerequisite of all criticism."[30] Hitchens also says, "Religious faith is, precisely *because* we are still-evolving creatures, ineradicable (emphasis in the original). It will never die out, or at least not until we get over our fear of death, and of the dark, and of the unknown, and of each other. For this reason," Hitchens concludes, "I would not prohibit it even if I thought I could."[31] On his judgment that religion is ineradicable, Hitchens is surely correct. As we shall see in chapter 5, when governments attempt to stamp out religious faith in the supernatural, it is almost invariably replaced by a political religion of far greater repressiveness than the supernatural faith it replaced.

In his own Four Horsemen gallop, Sam Harris seems to change targets midcourse between his first book and his second. As previously noted, it was the shock of the September 11 Islamic terrorist attacks that prompted Harris to write *The End of Faith* in the first place. Thus, his most detailed assault on any religion in this first book is on Islam, to which he devotes a lengthy and hard-hitting chapter. Many Christians and Jews would certainly enthusiastically agree with him in this chapter, recognizing readily that while the Koran has a few verses favoring toleration of other faiths, the vast weight of Koranic statements, the *hadith* (or private conversations) of Muhammed, and the central tradition of teaching about jihad advocate outright conquest of other faiths and the despotic rule of followers of those faiths once they have conceded defeat. In the rest of *The End of Faith*, Harris sallies forth against both Judaism and Christianity; he is an equal opportunity skeptic, though Christianity comes off marginally worse in the encounter because, as Harris—a secular Jew—is eager to remind everyone, for much of its history Christianity demonstrated cruelty and bigotry toward the Jews.

In his second book, *Letter to a Christian Nation*, however, Harris's target is quite specifically Christianity. Like Dawkins in *The God Delusion*, his aim is to "arm secularists in our society," though he also says, as noted in the previous chapter, that he has "set out to demolish the intellectual and moral pretensions of Christianity in its most committed forms."[32] Harris expresses doubt that he will succeed, and indeed he admits that the small book is itself "the product of failure—the failure of the many brilliant attacks upon religion that preceded it, the failure of our schools to announce the death of God in a way that each generation can understand, the failure of the media to criticize the abject religious certainties of our public figures—failures great and small that have kept almost every society on this earth muddling over God and despising those who muddle differently."[33] In short, Harris acknowledges, atheists have not done a good job of persuading people of the superiority of their point of view. Harris does not advocate explicit suppression of religious faith, but rather seeks what he calls "conversational intolerance." He explains, "When people make outlandish claims, without evidence, we stop listening to them—except on matters of faith. I am arguing that we can no longer afford to give faith a pass in this way."[34]

Behind that seemingly mild approach to religious belief, however, is a certain ruthlessness of viewpoint in Harris. He quite openly espouses the use of torture to elicit information from suspects in terrorism cases, describing it in *The End of Faith* as "not only permissible but necessary."[35] Even more chillingly, he also suggests that people espousing certain ideas that he considers truly harmful to society ought simply to be put to death.[36] More disturbing from the perspective of logic, throughout his two books Harris wields the saber of moral and ethical judgment as if there has never been any dispute among people of goodwill over what constitutes good and what constitutes evil. Harris overlooks the obvious point that the very concepts of good and evil came from a religious view of life, a view, moreover, that assumes that ordinary human beings have no difficulty in recognizing evil as evil or moral good as moral good when they see it. Without that moral consensus based on shared religious conviction, it is hard to see on what basis any group of humans can agree on what is or is not moral, beyond a handful of self-evident categories of reprehensible acts such as murder or cruelty to children. This, indeed, is one of the underlying philosophical weaknesses of the entire corpus of the Four Horsemen, and indeed of the entire New Atheism approach in general.

Much indignant rhetoric resounds through the works of these four writers as they point out the follies of religion and of religious belief, and indeed of the nature of God himself were he to exist (which, of course, according to the Four Horsemen, he obviously doesn't). But what is the source of that indignation? Dawkins and Dennett do engage in some sketchy speculation—and it is merely speculation—about the human origins of moral sentiments such as altruism. Harris is far more dogmatic: "We can easily think of objective sources of moral order that do not require the existence of a lawgiving God." He goes on:

> For there to be objective moral truths worth knowing, there need only be better and worse ways to seek happiness in this world. If there are psychological laws that govern human well-being, knowledge of these laws would provide an enduring basis for an objective morality.[37]

The multiple presumptions in these sentences are quite breath-taking. The subject of human happiness has challenged philosophers, priests, psychologists, and poets for millennia without yielding more than generalities as to what it consists of or how it is obtained. And "objective moral order" is to be based solely on human happiness? Whose happiness? And how is it measured? Is there to be a Gallup Poll conducted of the entire human race? And are the results to be published in the *New York Times*? Of all the Four Horsemen, Harris is easily the most philosophically confused. He says, for example, that "it is clearly possible to say that someone like Hitler was wrong in moral terms without reference to scripture."[38] True, but only because the German tyrant lost the war and the ideology of Nazism was discredited by the calamitous extent of the suffering it produced. Had Hitler won, Nazi racism and eugenics would have become the norm in all advanced societies, and Nazi propagandists would have said that their policies would lead to a more advanced, efficient, happier humankind. From whence then would come the "objective moral law" to declare this premise false?

Postmodernists have always said that morality is but the expression of power. If God doesn't exist, then the postmodernists are right and Sam Harris belongs to a quixotic minority of naysayers who speak as though absolutes existed, but who, in fact, don't believe in them.

Harris, to be sure, climbs out on a philosophical limb to places where none of his fellow Horsemen dare venture. There is, however, a consensus of propositions among these atheists that will be considered in detail in the following chapters. The arguments in the books of the Four Horsemen can be summed up as follows:

1. It is very improbable that God exists, and science can explain people's religious impulses.
2. Religions are bad because they cause people to do bad things, and most religious figures throughout history have been bad people.
3. If the God of the Jewish and Christian Scriptures existed, he would be a very bad person.
4. Science is everywhere and at all times opposed to religious belief.
5. Atheism (almost) never causes people to do bad things.
6. Most of America's Founding Fathers were deist, agnostic, or secular, and it is their Enlightenment understanding of society that forms the foundation of America's enduring freedom.
7. There is a dire civilizational need for atheism to prevail.

Starting in the next chapter, we examine—and criticize—these propositions. They will lead us in interesting directions.

# Chapter Three

# THEY
# DON'T LIKE GOD

*There was a young man who said, "God*
*Must think it exceedingly odd*
*If he finds that this tree*
*Continues to be*
*When there's no one about in the Quad."*

*Reply:*
*Dear Sir, Your astonishment's odd:*
*I am always about in the Quad.*
*And that's why this tree*
*Will continue to be,*
*Since observed by Yours faithfully, God*
— A limerick by Ronald Knox

This witty limerick by English theologian and priest Ronald Knox (who incidentally attended Balliol, the same Oxford college that both Richard Dawkins and Christopher Hitchens attended) sums up the philosophy of Bishop George Berkeley (1685–1753). Berkeley was one of the eighteenth century's most famous British philosophers and was known for the theory of "immaterialism," which holds that there are no material objects, only the mind and ideas. Others have called this view "subjective idealism."

Berkeley's philosophy recurred in the works of one of the most famous French philosophers of the past half century, Jean Baudrillard (1929–2007), who died in March 2007. One of Baudrillard's most famous (or infamous) works was his 1991 book, *The Gulf War Did Not Take Place*, in which he asserted that what appears to be reality to most people is actually only "simulacra," that is, various accumulated appearances of reality. Such was the 1991 Gulf War, for example, since it had no decisive political impact either in the United States or Iraq and was notable for the many TV newsclips of video-game-like footage showing "smart" bombs in combat.

Much more controversial was Baudrillard's 2002 book, *The Spirit of Terrorism: Requiem for the Twin Towers*, in which he suggested that the terrorist attacks of September 11 were largely a "dark fantasy" conjured up by the media. Though he acknowledged that the terrorists had indeed committed the atrocity, Baudrillard said it was simply the culmination of the savagery of modern bureaucratic living. This prompted one critic to write: "It takes a real demonic genius to brush off the slaughter of thousands on the grounds that they were suffering from severe *ennui* brought on by boring modern architecture."[1]

Baudrillard was also famous for another comment, one that is far more pertinent to our current discussion than the reality—or not—of the September 11 attacks. He said: "God exists, but I don't believe in him," which prompted Dawkins to coin a rather witty word for this sort of French philosophical pretentiousness: *francophonyism*. The put-down aside, Baudrillard's assertion can be usefully misquoted here to sum up the view that the Four Horsemen have of the Almighty: "God doesn't exist, and actually, I really don't like him either."

The overwhelming impression one gets from reading Dawkins, Dennett, Harris & Hitchens is that they are asserting the nonexistence of someone they sort of know—or at least think they know *about*—but whom they dislike venomously (especially true in the case of Dawkins), clandestinely admire (Daniel Dennett), or simply would not care to become acquainted with if he did exist (Hitchens and Sam Harris). So let's take a look at what it is about this God who doesn't exist that has gotten these four authors so worked up that each has gone to the considerable trouble and effort of writing hundreds of pages attacking him.

Dawkins is the most impassioned, and he positively quivers with rage in *The God Delusion* when talking about the Almighty. "The God of the Old Testament is arguably the most unpleasant character in all fiction," he thunders at the opening of his second chapter, "jealous and proud of it; a petty, unjust, unforgiving control-freak; a vindictive, bloodthirsty ethnic cleanser; a misogynistic, homophobic, racist, infanticidal, genocidal, filicidal, pestilential, megalomaniacal, sadomasochistic, capriciously malevolent bully." Having warmed up to a suitably feverish pitch, Dawkins winds up his opening paragraph for the prosecution of God with a zinger from Thomas Jefferson: "The Christian God is a being of terrific character—cruel, vindictive, capricious and unjust."

(Here it must be noted that the eighteenth-century meaning of *terrific* was "terrifying" rather than "great" or "wonderful.") As for that word *capricious,* since Jefferson used it first, then Dawkins *must* be right.[2]

But then, beginning the second paragraph, Dawkins has a spasm of self-doubt. "It is unfair to attack such an easy target," he concedes magnanimously. "The God Hypothesis should not stand or fall with its most unlovely instantiation, Yahweh, nor his insipidly opposite Christian face, 'Gentle Jesus meek and mild' . . . I am not attacking the particular qualities of Yahweh, or Jesus, or Allah, or any other specific god such as Baal, Zeus or Wotan."[3] (Oh? But didn't he just eviscerate Yahweh?) In case anyone still is unclear as to the targets of Dawkins's wrath, he summarizes himself a few pages later: "I am attacking God, all gods, anything and everything supernatural, wherever and whenever they have been or will be invented."[4] His target may be "all gods," but he keeps circling back to Yahweh. For Dawkins, the real villain is the deity of Judaism and Christianity.

How does he explain the problem of evil theologically? "Simply postulate a nasty god—such as the one who stalks every page of the Old Testament," he says.[5] Harris holds the same view: "The God of Abraham is a ridiculous fellow—capricious, petulant, and cruel—and one with whom a covenant is little guarantee of health or happiness."[6]

Dawkins goes further and personalizes the issue: "The God of the Bible is a real s—. . ."—well, that word should not appear in a family-friendly publication. Furthermore, since both Christianity and Islam anchor their own authenticity in the Old Testament narrative of patriarchs, kings, and prophets, Dawkins asserts—for the purposes of demolishing monotheism—that "all three Abrahamic religions can be treated as indistinguishable."[7] Let's consider briefly the awkward fact that it has been *only* in countries with a system of government profoundly influenced by Judaism or Christianity that monotheism can even be openly criticized at all; such criticism certainly is not tolerated in any country where Islam is dominant. If Dawkins had even let on in Taliban-ruled Afghanistan that he was merely *thinking* about writing *The God Delusion*, we would be reading his obituary now and not his book. Dawkins's inability or unwillingness to grasp how profoundly differently each of the three "Abrahamic" religious traditions evolved is perplexing, especially coming as it does from someone whose entire career has been spent studying evolution. He is loath to credit Christianity or Judaism with promoting tolerance or freedom of thought; yet, has anything even remotely atheist been published in any majority-Muslim country in the past two hundred years?

Dennett, by contrast, never gets as personal in his antitheistic campaign. In fact, he seems rather to admire the God of the Old Testament. "Part of what makes Jehovah such a fascinating participant in stories of the Old Testament," he writes, "is His kinglike jealousy and pride, and His great appetite for praise and sacrifices."[8] Unlike his three fellow Horsemen, Dennett—rather elegantly, in fact—refrains from the bombastic tirades that form the bulk of their attack on Old Testament Jewish beliefs and customs.

Not surprisingly, it is Dawkins who also leads the assault on events in the Old Testament. He provides a running commentary on barbarous goings-on, including a curiously detailed evocation of the story of Lot's two daughters getting him drunk so they could become pregnant by him (Genesis 19), as well as the events involving Lot and the citizens of Sodom (Genesis 19), Abraham being commanded to sacrifice his son Isaac (Genesis 22), Jephthah and his daughter (Judges 11), Aaron and the golden calf (Exodus 32), Moses and the Midianites (Numbers 25), and the Israelites and Jericho (Joshua 6). Dawkins denounces it all from the perspective of a twenty-first-century middle-class suburbanite: Abraham's willingness to sacrifice Isaac is "child abuse" and the "unfortunate Midianites" were "the victims of genocide in their own country."[9] Dawkins has no compunctions at all about passing judgment on degrees of sinfulness of these Old Testament events. The wickedness of "flirting with rival gods," for instance, is deemed "a trifling sin, compared to, say, offering your daughter for a gang rape."[10] The old man of Gibeah who provides hospitality to a visiting Levite and his concubine is, Dawkins declares, "misogynistic" when he tries to assuage the criminal lusts of the young men of Gibeah by giving them his own daughter and the visitor's concubine.[11]

Dawkins is after a larger point, though, and isn't merely highlighting those episodes of the Old Testament that seem cruel and even barbaric to the modern sensibility. "The point," he says, "is that, whether true or not, the Bible is held up to us as the source of our morality." Yet in this handbook of morality, Dawkins continues, the story of the destruction of Jericho and the invasion of the Promised Land are, in his view, "morally indistinguishable from Hitler's invasion of Poland, or Saddam Hussein's massacres of the Kurds and the Marsh Arabs."[12] He suggests that those who use the Bible as a moral guidebook don't even know all the sins for which, according to Leviticus 20, the perpetrator must be put to death: "cursing your parents; committing adultery; making love to your stepmother or your daughter-in-law; homosexuality; marrying a woman and her daughter; bestiality (and, to add injury to insult, the unfortunate beast is to be killed too)." Dawkins adds, "You also get executed, of course, for working on the sabbath: the point is made again and again throughout the Old Testament."[13]

Harris gets on a similar roll when attacking the Old Testament. "The idea that the Bible is a perfect guide to morality is simply astounding, given the contents of the book," he writes, citing some of the same death-penalty sins as Dawkins. He then devotes an entire page to an excerpt of Deuteronomy 13 about the necessity of putting to death anyone, whether he is a close family member or simply a member of the community, who seeks to entice the Israelites to worship foreign gods.[14] But wait; it gets worse. "Many Christians," Harris says, "believe that Jesus did away with all this barbarism in the clearest terms imaginable and delivered a doctrine of pure love and toleration.

He didn't," insists Harris. "In fact, at several points in the New Testament, Jesus can be read to endorse the entirety of Old Testament law."[15] He then quotes Jesus saying, "For truly, I say to you, till heaven and earth pass away, not an iota, not a dot, will pass from the law until all is accomplished. Whoever then relaxes one of the least of these commandments and teaches men so, shall be called least in the kingdom of heaven; but he who does them and teaches them shall be called great in the kingdom of heaven. For I tell you, unless your righteousness exceeds that of the scribes and Pharisees, you will never enter the kingdom of heaven" (Matthew 5:18–20, RSV).

Indeed, Harris is right that Jesus did not overturn the Old Testament law, but he has taken the two verses out of context and missed the greater point that Jesus was making in the entire passage, which begins in the previous verse: "Do not think that I have come to abolish the Law or the Prophets; I have not come to abolish them but to fulfill them" (NIV). Without that verse, the larger message is lost, which is that Jesus is declaring his intention to fulfill every jot and tittle of the Old Testament law and that, as Messiah, he would perfect the law. That being the case, then it only stands to reason that rather than invalidating the law, Jesus would endorse it so that he can build upon it, just as the U.S. Constitution has amendments that improve upon the original document. The amendments do not negate the Constitution any more than Jesus' teachings invalidated the Old Testament law. Rather, where the Old Testament law prohibits murder, for instance, Jesus in Matthew 5:21-22 prohibits anger; where the law forbids adultery, Jesus forbids lust, in Matthew 5:27-28.[16]

Hitchens's take on the barbarities of the Old Testament is entirely different from Harris's. He simply doesn't believe that any of it is historical fact. With customary panache, Hitchens dismisses it all: "It goes without saying that none of the gruesome, disordered events described in Exodus ever took place."[17] So rest easy, Sam and Richard, *none of it ever happened.* The last to join your gang assures us it's so.

As for the Bible's precepts, Hitchens is confident that they have long since been outdated by the cultural progress mankind has made since biblical times. He explains sarcastically: "The Bible may, indeed does, contain a warrant for trafficking in humans, for ethnic cleansing, for slavery, for bride-price, and for indiscriminate massacre, but we are not bound by any of it because it was put together by crude, uncultured human mammals."[18] (Hitchens has a peculiar habit in his writing of referring to people, from Japan's Emperor Hirohito to North Korean ruler Kim Il Sung, as "mammals." One reviewer described it as "a rhetorical tic.")

For Hitchens, it is the New Testament that most irritates, not the Old. No surprise that he calls the chapter of *God Is Not Great* dealing with this part of the Christian Bible "The 'New' Testament Exceeds the Evil of the 'Old' One." Hitchens revs up the same degree of indignation at the New Testament that Hawkins delivered at high volume against the Old Testament. Unfortunately, Hitchens, for all his literary learnedness and broad general knowledge of world events, is not exactly a scholar in New Testament hermeneutics, archaeology, culture, or textual criticism. In fact, he's completely out of his depth. So to whom does he turn for what he claims is an "irrefutably" accurate summation of the New Testament documents? Why, to a fellow-journalist, satirist, and atheist: the late H. L. Mencken (1880–1956).

Rather than choosing someone with respected academic credentials in biblical scholarship, Hitchens apparently thinks that Mencken is qualified to be an authority on the New Testament simply because of his well-known, vituperative animosity toward the fundamentalists of his day. And so he quotes Mencken declaring, "The simple fact is that the New Testament, as we know it, is a helter-skelter accumulation of more or less discordant documents, some of them probably of respectable origin but others palpably apocryphal, and that most of them, the good along with the bad, show unmistakable signs of having been tampered with." Hitchens alleges that Mencken's views and those of eighteenth-century freethinker Tom Paine "have been borne out by later biblical scholarship."[19] This bold claim of Hitchens, however, is supported by only a single source: the agnostic New Testament critic Bart Ehrman. Such a citation can hardly be considered representative of the body of "later biblical scholarship." (An examination of Ehrman's views of the reliability or unreliability of the New Testament is provided in the appendix.)

One more point needs to be made here, though, about

Hitchens's choice of Mencken as his voice of authority on the New Testament. In another part of his book, Hitchens refers to Mencken far more critically, saying that he's "too keen on Nietzsche," advocates social Darwinism and eugenics, and is "unpardonably indulgent" in his review of Adolf Hitler's manifesto and autobiography *Mein Kampf*. Though Hitchens doesn't mention it in *God Is Not Great*, he surely knows that Mencken was outspokenly anti-Semitic and that his diaries, published only in 1989, long after his death, were splattered with derogatory racist slurs toward both Jews and African Americans.

Having cited as an authority on the New Testament this notorious anti-Semite, Hitchens in the following paragraph turns his guns on the actor/producer Mel Gibson. The charge? *Anti-Semitism*. His poisonous characterization of Gibson would be startling to anyone not familiar with Hitchens's approach to opposition. In true Leninist fashion (Hitchens, after all, was indeed a Trotskyite at one point), he hurls at anyone he dislikes or who disagrees with him every destructive epithet a literary mind can seize on. Thus Gibson is "an Australian fascist and ham actor" who belongs to a "crackpot and schismatic Catholic sect" that Hitchens describes as "explicitly anti-Semitic." Of course, the real target of Hitchens's ire is Gibson's movie, *The Passion of the Christ*, which he says "sought tirelessly to lay the blame for the Crucifixion upon the Jews."[20] The movie was a huge commercial success and was, for millions of viewers, a profoundly moving depiction of the suffering of Jesus in his final hours of life. Its very popularity must have infuriated Hitchens.

In fairness to Hitchens, though, the charge of anti-Semitism against Gibson is not without basis. In the early morning of July 28, 2006, police on the Pacific Coast Highway in Malibu, California, pulled Gibson over for erratic driving and charged him with driving under the influence of alcohol, to which Gibson pled guilty. While he was being taken into custody, though, Gibson hurled some ugly, anti-Semitic slurs at the arresting officer, who indeed was Jewish. Gibson was universally criticized (and rightly so) for his outburst and later apologized profusely and repeatedly. (The Anti-Defamation League, which campaigns against anti-Semitism, rejected an apology by Gibson as "unremorseful," but later accepted a second, more effusive apology from him.)

Also in fairness to Hitchens, it should be noted that some Jewish organizations (as well as some Christian church groups) *did* object to *The Passion of the Christ* because they felt it portrayed the Jews as responsible for crucifying Jesus. (Many critics, however, including some Jewish critics, did not see it that way and thought the Romans came off as the major culprits.) In his diatribe against Gibson, Hitchens seems to have ignored an important difference between his hero, Mencken, and Gibson: Gibson publicly apologized for his anti-Semitic outburst; Mencken went to his grave an unrepentant bigot.

As the overview thus far of Dawkins's, Harris's, and Hitchens's views on the Bible has shown, one of the principal tactics of the New Atheists in their attack on God is to point to all the examples of cruelty that can be found in the Old Testament and thus discredit the Bible as far as possible in moral terms. That's harder to do with the New Testament, though, because it's well-known even by atheists that Jesus never killed or injured anybody, and, furthermore, that he went to his execution without resisting the authorities or instructing his disciples to oppose them. The most that can be made of a very weak case is to allege, as Harris does, that Jesus was endorsing in his teaching all of the barbarities of the Old Testament, or that the New Testament documents are so muddled and contradictory that none of the traditional Jesus story can really be relied upon anyway. That's a tack that Dawkins, Hitchens, and Harris all try. But as the sources provided in the bibliography show, serious biblical scholars suggest an entirely different approach.

The Four Horsemen don't just want to depict Jewish and Christian traditional beliefs as cruel or self-contradictory, though. They want to lay the charge that anyone, at any time, who has subscribed to these beliefs has either engaged in great wickedness or has been at risk of being provoked to do so by those beliefs. Harris, interestingly, devotes much more time in *The End of Faith* to denouncing Islamic zealotry than he does to the same danger posed by Christianity or Judaism; in so doing, he makes points that would hardly be contested by any Christian or Jewish readers. Suicide terrorism by Islamists, after all, has become a sad part of the American and global consciousness since September 11, 2001.

Harris, however, takes an odd tack that has been strongly criticized even by reviewers sympathetic to the atheist position.

He argues—and Dawkins seems to agree—that even moderate believers in any religion are dangerous, because the moderates provide legitimacy for their truly extreme vicious coreligionists. In *Letter to a Christian Nation*, Harris says: "Liberal and moderate Christians will not always recognize themselves in the 'Christian' I address . . . It is my hope, however, that they will also begin to see that the respect they demand for their own religious beliefs gives shelter to extremists of all faiths."[21] This thesis is developed at great length in *The End of Faith*, in which Harris points out the great dangers that expanding Islam has created for civilized life in the world.

Hitchens, of course, makes his position abundantly clear right on the cover of *God Is Not Great*. The subtitle says it all: *How Religion Poisons Everything*. Hitchens cannot bring himself to credit any religion, in any culture, at any time, with having a positive influence on humankind. Great works of Christian music, sculpture, literature—Bach's *Mass in B Minor* or his *St. Matthew Passion*, the Hagia Sophia church in Istanbul, Milton's *Paradise Lost*—or the magnificent architectural achievements of all the great religions are breezily dismissed as merely the results of civilizational and cultural advances that have nothing at all to do with faith. As he puts it, "When we read of the glories of 'Christian' devotional painting and architecture, or 'Islamic' astronomy and medicine, we are talking about advances of civilization and culture . . . that have as much to do with 'faith' as their predecessors had to do with human sacrifice and imperialism."[22] It takes a special kind of intellectual perversity, and indeed intellectual dishonesty, to make the claim that none of the great cultural achievements of the entire human race had *anything at all* to do with the religious sentiments of their creators. Has religion failed to create anything noble in the entire history of mankind? In the next sentence of his book, Hitchens reminds us that some of the purported religiously motivated creators may secretly have been atheists. So indeed they may have been, and indeed some probably were. But does the religious skepticism of a small minority of creative geniuses in the fields of religious art, music, literature, and architecture render invalid the faith convictions of the vast majority of the others? If Dawkins had an Anglo-Saxon equivalent of "franco-phonyism," it should be applied to this assertion by Hitchens. It's rather unlikely that any of the other Four Horsemen—as we shall see—feel this way.

Dawkins, Hitchens, and Harris do, however, share a common view when they point out some of the historical evils that can be laid squarely at the feet of people of faith, including, of course, Christians. Even the most devout religious believer has to agree that many outrages and barbarities in human history were religiously motivated in some way or other. To name the most obvious: the Crusades (chiefly because, on the way to Jerusalem and on their arrival there to *defend* the Christian holy places against Muslim persecution, "soldiers of the [Catholic] church" committed outrages against Jewish and Muslim communities) and the fifteenth-century Spanish Inquisition; the Roman Catholic persecution of the early Protestants (especially in France) in the sixteenth century and the subsequent English Protestant persecution of Roman Catholics; and spasms of anti-Semitism throughout Christian history. Christians must acknowledge all of them and, when possible, apologize for them.

Our own times are not without their examples of religious belief gone mad: the murderous clashes between Hindus and Muslims in South Asia and between Hindus and Buddhists in Sri Lanka; the bombings and killings in Northern Ireland by Catholics against Protestants, and vice versa; the sectarian religious warfare in Lebanon and Iraq; the ugly, religion-based ethnic cleansing in the Balkans. Hitchens luridly—even lovingly—documents his own experiences in some of the world's hot spots where sectarian violence has, indeed, been extreme. He even tells readers about instances of religious venom in places where the centrality of religion to the violence is not widely known. For example, few probably know what a key role Buddhism played in the aggression of Japanese militarism during World War II. Hitchens quotes the Japanese Buddhist leadership of the time, declaring, "We now have no choice but to exercise the benevolent forcefulness of 'killing one in order that many may live' (*issatsu tasho*). This is something which Mahayana Buddhism approves of only with the greatest of seriousness."[23]

Hitchens, Dawkins, and Harris also focus on the more recent iniquities of Islamic rage, including the violence that broke out in countries around the world and left at least 139 people dead after a Danish newspaper ran cartoons of Islam's prophet Muhammed, terrorist violence, and suicide bombings on buses in Israel, as well as Islamic terrorism in Spain, Morocco, India, Indonesia, and Britain. Few would disagree with Dawkins, Hitchens, and Harris about the link between religious fanaticism and these violent acts. Hitchens, however, goes further and is as extreme as the real religious extremists themselves in his rhetoric against all religious people. While he does not advocate violence of any kind against people of faith, nor, he says, would he support laws suppressing religious freedom, the extremist streak to Hitchens's discussion of religion seems to border on the pathological. His vicious characterization of Mel Gibson, who did indeed make ugly anti-Semitic comments for which he later apologized, is just one example. Here's an illustrative collection of the religious (and nonreligious) people Hitchens also skewers: St. Augustine, one of the most important church fathers of Western Christianity, is "a self-centered fantasist"; John Calvin, who developed the Reformed theology of Protestantism, is called "a sadist and a torturer and a killer"; the renowned Christian apologist and writer C. S. Lewis is "pathetic"; British journalist and late-in-life convert to Christianity Malcolm Muggeridge is deemed "silly"; and French Enlightenment writer and philosopher Voltaire is "ludicrous."

The religious figure who gets the worst of it, though, is Mother Teresa, and Hitchens is joined by Dawkins and Harris in some truly sharp personal attacks on her. This is old ground for Hitchens, whose 1995 book, *The Missionary Position: Mother Teresa in Theory and Practice*, is a full-bore attack on the Nobel Peace Prize–winning nun. Hitchens is proud of his distasteful and sophomoric title, because he says it is a triple entendre, as though the achievement of verbal cleverness always excuses a sneering sexual innuendo. In *God Is Not Great*, Hitchens calls her "an ambitious Albanian nun," but in *The Missionary Position* he is nastier, describing Mother Teresa as "the ghoul of Calcutta," "dangerous," "sinister," "fanatical," "an obscurantist," and "a demagogue."[24]

The basic material for the book was acquired for a BBC documentary called *Hell's Angel: Mother Teresa of Calcutta*. The documentary—and the book—noted that Mother Teresa had accepted donations from some rather shady sources, such as Haitian dictator "Papa Doc" Duvalier and American financier Charles Keating, who was convicted of fraud. Hitchens also criticized her for hobnobbing with some unpleasant political dictators in the Communist world, notably East German leader Erich Honecker and Albania's Maoist demagogue, Enver Hoxha. He could have added that when she arrived in South Africa on a visit before apartheid was abolished, she apparently didn't know that this system of racial segregation gave a white minority regime the right to rule over the black African majority. The documentary rounded up some disgruntled former volunteers for the Missionaries of Charity, the order Mother Teresa established, to tell unflattering stories about their standards of medicine and hygiene.

Mother Teresa was certainly naïve politically. Perhaps she was also, as Hitchens alleges, "cunning," in that she knew how to get financial support by appealing to the troubled consciences of powerful and wealthy people. No doubt the Missionaries of Charity have been negligent in disclosing details of their finances. But to point to these shortcomings in an attempt to negate Mother Teresa's life's work among the poorest of the poor of Calcutta and the rest of the world is totally missing the huge—and obvious—point. And that is that Mother Teresa literally picked up people abandoned to die on the streets and gave them a place to spend their last few days or hours on this earth in peace and dignity. In the early years, she sometimes used wheelbarrows and personally carted desperately ill people to local hospitals, where she simply refused to budge until they were treated.

A former leftist colleague of Hitchens said caustically of Hitchens's criticisms of Mother Teresa: "Between the two of them, my sympathies were with Mother Teresa. If you were sitting in rags in a gutter in Calcutta, who would be more likely to give you a bowl of soup?"[25]

It's no surprise that Dawkins and Harris dutifully repeat Hitchens's criticisms of Mother Teresa, as though the fact that a fellow-atheist has already picked on the Albanian nun opens the doors for atheists-in-waiting to do so as well. On the basis of Hitchens's book, Dawkins describes Mother Teresa as "sanctimoniously hypocritical" and having "cock-eyed judgment" (for saying that "the greatest destroyer of peace is abortion").[26]

Harris quotes Hitchens on Mother Teresa's identification with poverty, and speaks approvingly of his "characteristic bluntness" in disparaging it. But Harris at least has the decency to admit the obvious, that "there is no denying that Mother Teresa was a great force for compassion."[27]

The oddest, and surely most intellectually indefensible, aspect of Hitchens's entire book is his refusal to concede a grain of religious conviction or authenticity to people he admires as humanitarians but who happened to be people motivated profoundly by their Christian faith. Hitchens admires greatly, as well he might, German Lutheran pastor Dietrich Bonhoeffer (1906–1945), who was hanged by the Nazis. According to Hitchens, Bonhoeffer was executed because "he refused to collude with them."[28] That's just Hitchens's lazy interpretation of a far more complex situation, an interpretation that completely ignores Bonhoeffer's faith.

Bonhoeffer was hanged by the Nazis in the prison of Flossenberg just three weeks before the end of World War II because of his connection with anti-Hitler elements in the German military intelligence, or *Abwehr*. He had been arrested in April 1943 after funds to help Jews escape to Switzerland were traced back to him. When a plot to assassinate Hitler was foiled, Bonhoeffer's fate was sealed because the conspirators were all associates of his. In essence, Bonhoeffer was hanged because he was believed to be connected with the plot to murder Hitler.

Hitchens explains Bonhoeffer's defiance of Hitler and his

formidable courage during imprisonment as stemming from "nebulous humanism" and not from faith. After all, he asserts, "Religion spoke its last intelligible or noble or inspiring words a long time ago: either that or it mutated into an admirable but nebulous humanism."[29] And how was this "nebulous humanism" evident in the last few hours of Bonhoeffer's life? Ten years later, the camp doctor at Flossenberg, who had witnessed the behavior of all of the condemned prisoners of the Nazis on the day before each was executed, wrote this of Bonhoeffer:

> Through the half-open door in one room . . . , I saw Pastor Bonhoeffer, before taking off his prison garb, kneeling on the floor praying fervently to his God. I was most deeply moved by the way this lovable man prayed, so devout and so certain that God heard his prayer.[30]

After describing the courage and composure Bonhoeffer exhibited at his hanging, the doctor wrote, "In the almost fifty years that I worked as a doctor, I have hardly ever seen a man die so entirely submissive to the will of God."[31] Later in the book, Hitchens grudgingly admits that "many Christians gave their lives to protect their fellow creatures in this midnight of the century." Then, quite incredibly, he trivializes their faith, their conscience, and their courage, dismissing it all with the snide observation that it "is statistically almost negligible" that they were following "orders from any priesthood."[32] By this he means that unless a person is obeying the orders of his priest when he acts courageously, the faith component of his life is irrelevant. Let's see now, it's virtually impossible for any person of faith in any age or any circumstance to demonstrate courage unless ordered to do so by a priest, right? So many examples of Christians acting with great courage without a priest in sight can be found throughout history that it is quite amazing that Hitchens, despite being very well read, seems entirely ignorant of them.

An excellent example is Bonhoeffer's fellow German contemporary Helmuth James von Moltke (1907–1945) who, like Bonhoeffer, paid with his life for resistance to the Nazis. Unlike Bonhoeffer, von Moltke, the scion of a distinguished Prussian military family, took part in no plots against Hitler. He was hanged by the Nazis purely and simply because of his faith; a kangaroo-court trial convicted him of treason based on his Christian beliefs. In his final letter to his wife, in January 1945, he rejoiced that he was not involved in the same putsch against Hitler in which Bonhoeffer was implicated. The reason for this? If he was going to be executed, he wanted it to be solely for his Christian faith, not because of his political dissent. Von Moltke explained to his wife in this deeply moving letter that "the decisive stage of the trial" was when he addressed the Nazi judge who had said, "One thing Christianity and we National Socialists have in common, and only one: we demand the whole man." [33] Then he wrote,

> Your husband is chosen, as a Protestant, to be above all attacked and condemned for his friendship with Catholics,

and therefore he stands before Freisler [the presiding judge] not as a Protestant, not as a big landowner, not as a nobleman, not as a Prussian, not as a German but as a Christian and nothing else. "The fig leaf is off," says Herr Freisler. Yes, every other category was removed.[34]

Hitchens finds it impossible to believe that religious people might, just occasionally, be motivated by faith to do something good in the world, and his blind bigotry is not confined just to those dark days of World War II in Europe. He casts equal aspersions on more recent American heroes. To his credit, Hitchens does hold in high regard a handful of people whom most Americans also admire for their courage and historical contribution to American society. One of them, not surprisingly, is American civil rights leader Martin Luther King Jr. Hitchens, in a rare moment of vulnerability, writes, "It is quite impossible even for an atheist like myself to read his sermons or watch recordings of his speeches without profound emotion of the sort that can sometimes bring genuine tears."[35] He eloquently describes King's ability to speak of the rights of African Americans in terms reminiscent of the Hebrew prophets. Then he knowingly tells his readers, "Christian reformism arose originally from the ability of its advocates to contrast the Old Testament with the New."[36] That explanation would probably surprise everyone from Martin Luther, who launched the Protestant Reformation, to William Wilberforce, who devoted his life to ending Britain's slave trade.

But never mind. Having embarked on this shabby attempt to explain why Christians have so often been at the forefront of social activism, Hitchens can't help lurching off for several paragraphs to rant about the teachings of John the Baptist and Jesus on heaven and hell. He links this digression to his commentary on King by declaring that those biblical teachings couldn't have anything to do with what the civil rights leader believed because King never called down punishment, earthly or heavenly, on his persecutors. For this failure to preach hell and damnation, King is also relegated by Hitchens to the ranks of nonbelievers with this summary judgment: "In no real as opposed to nominal sense, then, was he a Christian."[37]

This would certainly be news to all the African Americans who worked closely with King, who were with him when he was assassinated, or who continue to revere his name. Hitchens's pronouncement is based on a curiously blinkered view of King's life, one that ignores, for instance, the fact that this ordained Baptist minister was the one who gave the civil rights movement its slogan, "Thou shalt not requite violence with violence." Or the fact that King was so well known for his advocacy of nonviolent protest that he has been likened to Gandhi, and that he was awarded the Nobel Peace Prize not only for leading the civil rights movement but also for his exemplary role as peacemaker. In fact, the Nobel Prize Committee, in announcing his 1964 award, referred explicitly to King's faith: "Martin Luther King's belief is rooted first and foremost in the teachings of Christ" and cited King's 1955 speech in which he exhorted protestors, "Our actions must be guided by the deepest principles of Christian faith. . . . Once again we must hear the words of Jesus echoing across the centuries: 'Love your enemies, bless them that curse you, and pray for them that despitefully use you.'"[38]

This question of whether King was a Christian came up in a generally well-mannered debate between Hitchens and Rev. Al Sharpton in May 2007 at the New York Public Library. Sharpton, who is close to some of King's associates and who had served as youth director of an organization with close ties to King, gave this unequivocal answer: "In terms of the civil rights movement, it was absolutely fueled by a belief in God and a belief in right or wrong. Had not there been this belief that there was a right and a wrong, the civil rights movement . . . would not have existed. . . . There is no question that [King] himself saw that the basis of the movement was God-based. To try and secularize the civil rights movement is totally inaccurate. It was a church-based, faith-based movement; there's just no question about that. . . . Let's not reinvent Dr. King any more than we try to reduce God to some denomination or convention."[39]

It's a shame that so eloquent and in many ways effective a voice for atheism as Hitchens, someone who has shown genuine moral courage in certain situations, should be reduced to such specious reasoning as to deny Christian convictions to one of the most heroic figures in American history.

Was King flawed in his personal life? Yes, he was. He was a

sinner, as all Christians admit they are by their very decision to believe in Jesus as Savior. For Hitchens, however, to attempt to cast King as another flag carrier for "nebulous humanism" is not just plain wrong, it's frankly dishonest. Hitchens doesn't even have to resort to this sleight of hand. There are plenty of bad eggs in the history of Christianity. What's deeply saddening is that someone of Hitchens's considerable eloquence, learning, and intelligence should be so deeply bigoted against faith as to deny that there are any good eggs. Perhaps Dawkins would not leave us bereft of a neologism after all: *Anglophonyism*—based on the fact that Hitchens is British born and educated.

The basic cry of the New Atheists, as of the old atheists, is that they hate God. They claim not to believe that he exists, but their animosity is so personal that it is hard to escape the conclusion that they are combating a personality who in some intuitive way they know is real. God is really horrible, say the Four Horsemen, but, darn it, we can't ignore him. Father of Communism Karl Marx seemed to swing this way when he desperately attempted to do away with the deity in his search for the laws of history. Marx called his ideas "scientific socialism," a speculative utopia based on a claim that he alone had uncovered the scientific principles governing history.

The Four Horsemen hold science in similarly high regard, as we'll see. Dawkins, the only scientist among them, seems to believe that all the serious dilemmas besetting the human condition can be dealt with effectively by the application of the scientific method. It's a little reminiscent of the formula

proposed by his twentieth-century predecessor among professional atheists, Bertrand Russell: "The good life is one inspired
by love and guided by knowledge."[40] Dawkins's twenty-first-
century concoction: the deification of science in the form of
"scientism."

# Chapter Four

# THE

# SCIENCE PROBLEM

*"In this modern era of cosmology, evolution, and the human*
*genome, is there still the possibility of a richly satisfying*
*harmony between the scientific and spiritual worldviews?"*
— Francis Collins in *The Language of God*

Two of the Four Horsemen came to their atheism early in life through childhood experiences that led to an unbeliever's equivalent of an "epiphany." Richard Dawkins had been brought up in the Anglican Church, but when he was about nine years old, he realized that there were many religions and that they couldn't all be true.[1] Christopher Hitchens, also at about age nine, was disgusted with his primary school teacher, a Mrs. Watts, when she brought God into her lessons about nature. Acting as both teacher and Sunday school instructor, she taught her young charges that God had made the trees and grass green because that was the color most restful for human eyes. "I was frankly appalled by what she said," the middle-aged Hitchens recalls of that earlier outburst of his choleric nature. "I simply *knew* . . . that my teacher had managed to get everything wrong in just two sentences" (emphasis in the original).

What Hitchens "knew" was that "the eyes were adjusted to nature, and not the other way about," he explains in his book, with no scientific sources to back up the statement.[2]

Daniel Dennett was brought up in the lukewarm, conviction-lite Congregationalism of New England (today as famously indifferent to Christianity—with the definite exception of some individual churches—as it was zealous for it three and a half centuries ago). He says he realized when he was a teenager that the interest he'd had all along in religion was "academic—I didn't believe it at all."[3] As for Sam Harris, whatever faith in a deity he might have ever had seems to have been leached out of his soul between his hallucinogenic experience with the drug "ecstasy" in 1986 and his deep plunges into meditation in India and the United States in the eleven years following. In a long chapter at the end of *The End of Faith* called "Experiments in Consciousness," Harris discourses on meditation, mysticism, "consciousness," and awareness of the self. He quotes at some length the Indian Buddhist mystic Padmasambhava, also known as the Guru Rinpoche, who is credited with bringing Tantric Buddhism to Tibet in the mid-eighth century. Padmasambhava is revered as the patron saint of the Himalayan state of Sikkim, now part of India, and regarded by some followers as the second Buddha.

Harris rambles off into a euphoric rhapsody about Eastern meditation, offering his learned opinion that "when the great philosopher mystics of the East are weighed against the patriarchs of the Western philosophical and theological traditions, the difference is unmistakable: Buddha, Shankara, Padmasambhava, Nagarjuna, Longchenpa, and countless others down to the present have no equivalents in the West. In spiritual terms, we appear to have been standing on the shoulders of dwarfs."[4] Harris's paean to Eastern mysticism prompted one reviewer of *The End of Faith* to comment, "The dirty little secret of that book is that Harris turns out to be a Buddhist."[5] Atheists need fear no heart palpitations over this astounding revelation: Many Buddhists have themselves described Buddhism as atheistic.

Of the Four Horsemen, Dawkins is the one who launches the most vigorous assault upon religion and belief in God. Of course, all the Horsemen cite numerous examples of the alleged wickedness of religious faith, but Dawkins more than the others focuses on what makes belief in God, in his view, inherently mistaken. He comes at it from several different positions, in the process attacking everyone from Saint Thomas Aquinas to the Dalai Lama. The main thrust, however, is the argument that science is the answer to everything. Each of the Four Horsemen, with the possible exception of Hitchens, seems to share this approach. All four seem to think that science has so completely explained the known universe that there is no room to view life's realities outside the rigidly defined parameters of the scientific method. Although Dawkins is the most extreme in his declaration of "scientism," at heart, all Four Horsemen seem to have constructed this same arid universe wherein dwells no God, no transcendence, no mystery other than what can be conjured from contemplating physical nature—and an ill-tempered intolerance of anyone who suggests otherwise.

Dawkins's approach was originally laid out in the first of his books to achieve significant success, *The Selfish Gene* (1976), which launched a minirevolution of thinking in the area of genetics.[6] In *The Selfish Gene*, Dawkins introduced the term *meme*, a name for a unit of cultural information that is transmitted in a manner analogous to genes; that is, a *meme* is the equivalent in the world of ideas and culture to a *gene* in the world of natural science. Genes have long been accepted by the scientific community as the linchpins of the evolutionary process, acting as biological replicators to pass on to their host's future generations the genetic information necessary to propel evolution forward. Dawkins came up with the term *meme* for the mechanism that he speculated conveys cultural attributes, including belief in God, from phenotype to phenotype (i.e., the host animal—in this case, human beings). He gives as examples of "meme" such things as catchphrases, clothing fashions, and beliefs.

It needs to be said that the meme is entirely a speculative entity. No scientist has ever found a way to observe one or measure it, much less reproduce its likeness in a laboratory setting. It is an alluring theory of cultural change, but its existence has never been proved. The theory of "memetics" is a proto-science, some might say a pseudoscience. It might not be too unkind to compare memetics with "phlogiston theory," a now entirely defunct scientific hypothesis dating to the second half of the seventeenth century that attempted to explain oxidation processes. The theory was discredited only when the French chemist Antoine Lavoisier (1743–1794), known as the father of modern chemistry and a codiscoverer of hydrogen and oxygen, stated the law of conservation of mass.

Lavoisier is also relevant to this discussion of atheism because, despite his impeccable Enlightenment credentials, he was put to death during the French Revolution's Reign of Terror by the first atheist regime in modern history, the National Convention. It accused him of being a traitor because he had held a post in the government of the monarchy that had been overthrown by the revolution. Anticipating Lenin, Mao, and Pol Pot, the head of the Revolutionary Tribunal that sentenced him to guillotining said, "La République n'a pas besoin de savants," meaning the republic had no need of scientists.[7]

Despite the fragile basis for the meme idea, such has been the prestige of Dawkins that the theory has taken on a life of its own and developed its own school of adepts. One of its earliest and most ardent advocates, not surprisingly, is fellow Horseman Daniel Dennett, who elaborated on the meme in two books, *Consciousness Explained* (1991) and *Darwin's Dangerous Idea* (1995). We will look more closely at Dennett's contribution to the Four Horsemen debate later in this chapter. For now, let's see how an insoluble contradiction involving religion almost stumps Dawkins in *The God Delusion*. According to most widely accepted explanations of evolution, animal behavior is almost always determined by the need for group survival, and survival requires the greatest economy in the use of resources. Dawkins, however, sees a particular problem with religion: It is "so wasteful, so extravagant; and Darwinian selection habitually targets and eliminates waste."[8] How to square the circle? "What is it all for?" he asks of the acts of sacrifice and the killing that have been done in the name of religion. "What is the benefit of religion?"[9]

Dawkins answers his own question by a fertile burst of speculation: Since humans seem to derive no obvious benefit from religion—of course not, or Dawkins wouldn't be an atheist—perhaps it exists to benefit not our genes but the survival of religion itself. As Dawkins puts it: "It may be to the benefit of only the religious ideas themselves, to the extent that they behave in a somewhat gene-like way, as replicators."[10] In other words, religious ideas, because they are memes, which in Dawkins's theory are cultural analogues of biological genes, have adopted a "circle the wagons" strategy to protect themselves from attack by the memes of atheism or criticism.

Another explanation, which Dawkins doesn't suggest, is the possibility that the religion memes have discovered that religious faith reduces stress in human beings, thus providing the memes with a more stable phenotype. That is to say, perhaps churchgoing Christians make more hospitable hosts. An abundance of scientific research has concluded that people who are regular churchgoers or who otherwise engage regularly in religious activities live longer than those who do not,[11] but Dawkins's distaste for Christianity in any form is so extreme that he can barely stomach this idea. "It is hard to believe, for example," he says with characteristic disdain, "that health is improved by the semi-permanent state of morbid guilt suffered by a Roman Catholic possessed of normal human frailty and less than normal intelligence. Perhaps it is unfair to single out the Catholics," he says, succumbing to a rare paroxysm of fairness. But then the knife comes out again, in the form of a quote from an American comedian that "religion is basically guilt, with different holidays."[12]

Dawkins elaborates his meme theory with digressions to the famous "cargo cult" religions of Pacific Melanesia. The origins of these religions are very recent, certainly no later than just before or during World War II, when American soldiers and support personnel descended on the hitherto extremely backward Melanesian societies with advanced technology and, above all, transport aircraft that delivered cargo seen by the natives to be valuable. Hoping to entice cargo planes to bring to their own tribes a similar cornucopia of food and supplies, the natives constructed from local materials facsimiles of radio masts, crude representations of aircraft, and even a makeshift "runway." The deities that delivered goods from the sky, the tribespeople presumed, might be attracted by the appearance of things on the ground that had brought the original cargo planes in.

On the island of Tanna in present-day Vanuatu, formerly the New Hebrides, one such cult continues to survive, focused on a messianic mythical figure the locals call "John Frum." Whether a real John Frum ever existed isn't clear, though if he did in some form or other, he evidently was a white man who might have been an American serviceman. The cult, however, turned anarchic in 1941, when a native leader of the John Frum religion began to prophesy apocalyptic events and the eventual return of John Frum. Natives were instructed to abandon Christianity, spend all the white man's money, and retreat to an inland part of the island to resume their ancient traditions.

The atheists seem to be especially fascinated by the cargo cults, and Hitchens, Dawkins, and Dennett all mention them, with the latter two devoting considerable verbiage to the subject. It isn't difficult to see why: The cargo cults were belief systems based on real events (the arrival of American servicemen during World War II with cargo planes, rifles, and seemingly endless quantities of supplies) from which a messianic belief developed (a savior figure named John Frum would eventually return to the islands and inaugurate peace and prosperity for all). Dawkins notes in a footnote that the tendency to believe in a messiah figure "doesn't necessarily indicate any fundamental feature of the human psyche, or Jungian 'collective unconscious.'" He explains with characteristic revulsion, "These islands had long been infested with missionaries."[13] To Dawkins, "missionary" equals "vermin," and his hostility toward Christians is as real as rat poison. The clear intention of the Horsemen in zeroing in on the cargo cults is to imply that Christianity developed in the same way these cults did: in a wacky atmosphere of delusions about events for which there are, supposedly, perfectly rational explanations.

Dennett, in fact, turns this comparison into a minisermon by which a blessedly brainy academic atheist begins to relieve simpleminded people of faith of their delusions. "Your religion, you may believe," he says, not with Dawkins's malice but with oleaginous condescension, "came into existence when its fundamental truth was revealed by God to somebody, who then passed it along to others. It flourishes today because you and the others of your faith know that it is the truth, and God has blessed you and encouraged you to keep the faith. It is as simple as that, for you."[14] This is one of many examples where Dennett talks down to those readers who are religious believers. His relentlessly condescending tone prompted one reviewer to comment: "Dennett's style in this book resembles nothing more than a leftist pamphlet, aimed at the masses but read by the already converted, patiently explaining in dumbed-down style what all reasonable people ought to know anyway. The result is the same sermonizing tone you'll find in the worst Communist pamphlets."[15]

In Dawkins's hands, the cargo cults are used to "prove" his meme theory of the development of religion, and he explains this theory at some length. In fairness to Dawkins, he offers his meme theory of religion as a work in progress, as well he might, considering that the validity of memetic theory is still being debated.[16] "The central question for meme theory," Dawkins argues, "is whether there are units of cultural imitation which behave as true replicators, like genes. I am not saying that memes necessarily *are* close analogues of genes, only that the more like genes they are, the better will meme theory work; and the purpose of this section is to *ask* whether meme theory might work for the special case of religion" (emphasis in the original).[17] It becomes clear as one reads the meme section of *The God Delusion* how tentative Dawkins is about it all. He admits that "the meme pool is less structured and less organized than the gene pool. Nevertheless," he insists, "it is not obviously silly to speak of a meme pool, in which particular memes might have a 'frequency' which can change as a consequence of competitive interactions with alternative memes."[18]

But if memes are as real as Dawkins alleges, why is there so much uncertainty about them? Dawkins isn't even clear in his own mind how to designate different categories of memes. "Do memes exist only in brains?" he asks. "Or is every paper copy and electronic copy of, say, a particular limerick also entitled to be called a meme? Then again, genes replicate with very high fidelity, whereas, if memes replicate at all, don't they do so with low accuracy?" Dawkins answers his own question: "These alleged problems of memes are exaggerated. The most important objection is the allegation that memes are copied with insufficiently high fidelity to function as Darwinian replicators."[19] Dawkins acknowledges that the scientific community has doubts about the meme idea: "Another objection is that we don't know what memes are made of, or where they reside. Memes have not yet found their Watson and Crick; they lack even their Mendel. Whereas genes are to be found in precise locations on chromosomes, memes presumably exist in brains and we have even less chance of seeing one than of seeing a gene."[20]

Alister McGrath, an Oxford theologian who earned a doctorate in molecular biophysics before turning to theology, makes this dry observation in *Dawkins' God:* "Dawkins talking about memes is like believers talking about God—an invisible, unverifiable postulate, which helps explain some things about experience, but ultimately lies beyond empirical investigation."[21]

These questions notwithstanding, Dawkins takes the meme idea into the area of different religions. Just as some genes do better in certain gene pools—carnivore genes would not thrive, for instance, in an herbivore gene pool—so some memes survive, Dawkins says, only in the presence of certain other memes. He proposes the idea that "Islam is analogous to a carnivorous gene complex, Buddhism to a herbivorous one." For Dawkins, "the strong possibility remains that the detailed form of each religion has been largely shaped by unconscious evolution." At advanced stages of the evolution of religions, the unique features of various religions can be explained by the Dawkins "theory of memeplexes—cartels of mutually compatible memes." At the end of the paragraph, though, Dawkins offers a throwaway line that all but contradicts his foregoing meme theory. "This doesn't rule out," he concludes, "the additional role of deliberate manipulation by priests and others. Religions probably are, at least in part, intelligently designed, as are schools and fashions in art."[22]

If memes are to be taken seriously, might there not be a meme for religious skepticism? Or, as McGrath posits, a meme for belief in memes? If so, McGrath concludes, "The meme concept then dies the slow death of self-referentiality, in that, if taken seriously, the idea explains itself as much as anything else."[23]

Well, precisely. It is curious how inattentive Dawkins is to anthropological and sociological theories of the origins of religion. He does, to be sure, mention Sir James Frazer, whose *The Golden Bough: A Study in Religion and Magic* sought to explain much of early religious belief as magic. But Frazer's work, while impressive for its day (the thirteen-volume work was published over two decades beginning in 1890) and deeply influential on several generations of critics of religion, has been criticized more recently for its serious flaws. For example, Frazer relied on anecdotes from missionaries and travelers for some of his evidence. He also held to superficial interpretations of cultural evolution, most of which were discarded in the twentieth century when a consensus arose that the human mind is infinitely more varied in its operation than Frazer believed and that religion probably did not develop in all societies following a universal pattern. Nonetheless, Dawkins soldiers on.

"The general theory of religion as an accidental byproduct—a misfiring of something useful—is one I wish to advocate," he writes. "The details," he admits, "are various, complicated, and disputable."[24] The details essentially boil down to one of Dawkins's pet explanations of religion: It's a mental virus, you see, that flits from brain to brain, infecting new generations of children, who, once they have grown up, pass the infection on to the next generation. According to Dawkins, there is probably a "god-meme" which is powerful, replicates itself in the mind, and has high survival traits (presumably including an ability to resist Dawkins's theories). But doesn't that suggest that, if there is a "god-meme," there should also be an "atheism-meme"? If Dawkins's meme theory has any validity at all, then the process by which people come to believe in atheism as the best explanation of the universe must be analogous to his theory of religion memes flitting across human culture and infecting people. Dawkins addresses this, but then dismisses it with a remarkable example of special pleading: "Scientific ideas, like all memes, are subject to a kind of natural selection, and this might look superficially virus-like. But the selective forces that scrutinize scientific ideas are not arbitrary or capricious. They are exacting, well-honed rules, and they do not favor pointless, self-serving behavior."[25]

Dawkins might as well have also asserted that scientists are quite immune from competitive urges, envy, selfish ambition, and the tendency to squabble with people perceived to be rivals in the scientific community—in fact, immune from every vice that afflicts the rest of the human race. And if you buy that, you might also be interested in buying some oceanfront property in Montana.

Dennett takes up the notion of religion as a virus very early in *Breaking the Spell.* He employs the colorful analogy of the lancet fluke, which must find its way into a sheep or cow to complete its reproductive cycle. That is why, when it has taken over the brain of an ant, it compels the poor ant to keep climbing to the top of every blade of grass it can find in order to be devoured by a cow or sheep. In the same way, Dennett suggests, viruses of various religious systems lodge themselves in our brains and cause us to behave in ways that often don't make sense to outsiders. Unlike Dawkins and Hitchens, who slash away at religion, particularly Christianity, as though it were thick jungle undergrowth getting in the way of reaching the holy grail of atheism, Dennett's entire book is based on the premise that religion needs to be studied as a natural phenomenon and that religious believers oppose such study.

"It is high time," he says portentously, "that we subject religion as a global phenomenon to the most intensive multidisciplinary research we can muster, calling on the best minds on the planet." We must do so, says Dennett, "because religion is too important for us to remain ignorant about."[26] Dennett spends much of the remainder of his book trying to demonstrate that there has been a taboo against the scientific study of religions, a "spell" that must be broken—hence the book's title. Dennett even sees himself as a revivalist preacher for atheism. "I say unto you," he declaims, mimicking revivalist fervor, "O religious folks who fear to break the taboo: Let go! Let go! You'll hardly notice the drop!"[27] One hesitates to ask whither the religious folk, having abandoned their "taboo," will drop. Is it onto a patch of thick carpeting just a few inches below their feet or through the trapdoor of a gallows?

The one emphatic thought that Dennett wishes to leave with

readers is that religion is quite often "belief in belief," a point that Dawkins picks up on with alacrity. Dennett has an entire chapter with this very title, and he summarizes the content in this paragraph:

> Many people believe in God. Many people believe in *belief in God*. What's the difference? People who believe in God are sure that God exists, and they are glad, because they hold God to be the most wonderful of all things. People who moreover believe in belief in God are sure that *belief in God* exists (and who could doubt that?), and they think that this is a good state of affairs, something to be strongly encouraged and fostered wherever possible: If only *belief in God* were more widespread! (emphasis in the original)[28]

"It is entirely possible to be an atheist and believe in belief in God," Dennett says in the next paragraph, as though that were surprising, given that the notion of "belief in belief" is entirely of his own (atheistic) concocting.[29] Dennett, though, is just such an atheist, one who holds to the notion of "belief in belief," and he is not alone. Most Christians have had the experience of an agnostic or atheist commenting rather wistfully, "I wish I had your faith." But Dennett reduces faith to a flat, rationalistic assent to certain doctrinal propositions.

John Gray, professor of European thought at the London School of Economics, in a *New Statesman* review delightfully titled "Atheists are irrational too," writes, "In fixating on the belief-content of religion, Dennett emulates Christianity at its most rationalistic and dogmatic," and observes that "there is more scepticism in a single line of the *Pensees* [the defense of Christianity by the seventeenth-century philosopher and mathematician Blaise Pascal] than in the whole of Dennett's leaden tome."[30]

Though easy to read, it is leaden indeed. Dennett is rambling, discursive, sometimes informative and entertaining, but he at least, of all the Four Horsemen, seems to have spent some time in the company of believers and not, à la Hitchens, pinning them to the wall with the flaming daggers of his debating skills. Dennett is therefore not sharply offensive to religious believers in the way that Dawkins and Hitchens are. Yet reviewers were far more intensely critical of Dennett's book than of the other Four Horsemen's. The introduction to Gray's review observed, "To many atheists, religion is no more than a form of magical thinking hard-wired into us by evolution. But they are mistaken in assuming their own view to be any more rational. The need for myths fuels secular beliefs, too." Gray explains further, "The chief difference between religious and secular believers is that, while the former have long known their myths to be extremely questionable, the latter imagine their own to be literally true."[31]

Perhaps more tellingly, another reviewer laments that Dennett doesn't introduce into his book any commentary from the humanities or social sciences. "The most striking gap in

*Breaking the Spell*," wrote science historian and journalist John Cornwell in Britain's *The Sunday Times*, "is its lack of humanistic commentary from anthropology, aesthetics, and confessional literature. . . . *Breaking the Spell* is an insidious book; not because it breaks taboos by asking uncomfortable questions of religion, nor because its author is an ardent atheist, but because it is written by a brilliant philosopher who betrays his academic standards by proceeding from emotive, ill-informed prejudice."[32]

Dennett holds to the same "scientism" that we've already encountered in Dawkins: a worldview that refuses to concede any limitations whatsoever to the sciences. In a February 2006 *New York Times* review of *Breaking the Spell*, Leon Wieseltier, literary critic for *The New Republic*, hammered mercilessly at this aspect of Dennett's approach to reality. "Scientism," he wrote, "the view that science can explain all human conditions and expressions, mental as well as physical, is a superstition, one of the dominant superstitions of our day; and it is not an insult to science to say so. . . . *Breaking the Spell* is a work of considerable historical interest, because it is a merry anthology of contemporary superstitions."[33]

Dawkins, in fact, was outraged when fellow evolutionist, the late Harvard University professor Stephen Jay Gould, in his book *Rocks of Ages*, proposed that Darwinian evolution left entirely open the issue of whether or not God existed. Gould, who was as ardent an exponent of Darwinian evolutionism as Dawkins and was an agnostic, wrote: "Either half my colleagues are enormously stupid, or else the science of Darwinism is fully compatible with conventional religious beliefs—and equally compatible with atheism."[34]

In *Rocks of Ages*, Gould advanced a view that has been strongly criticized both by Dawkins and some Christians, though for differing reasons. It is referred to—and, of course, attacked in *The God Delusion*—as NOMA, or "non-overlapping magisteria," borrowing from the Roman Catholic term *magisterium* meaning, "the authority to teach religious doctrine." In essence, Gould held that the "magisterium" of science dealt only with the empirical realm, whereas religion dealt with "questions of ultimate meaning." Some Christians in science, such as Francis Collins, director of the National Human Genome Research Institute, and Oxford's Alister McGrath, disagree with Gould's formulation, insisting that science and faith can—and should—work together and that they are not two separate realms having nothing to do with each other.

Dawkins, for his part, seems almost out of control with frustration at Gould's formulation. "I simply do not believe that Gould could possibly have meant much of what he wrote in *Rocks of Ages*," he writes.[35] Dawkins refers to *Rocks of Ages* as "one of [Gould's] less admired books" because in it Gould "carried the art of bending over backwards to positively supine lengths."[36] To illustrate his point he quotes McGrath quoting Gould: "To say it for all my colleagues and for the umpteenth millionth time (from college bull sessions to learned treatises):

science simply cannot (by its legitimate methods) adjudicate the issue of God's possible superintendence of nature. We neither affirm nor deny it."[37] Although Dawkins rhetorically wonders, "What are these ultimate questions in whose presence religion is an honoured guest and science must respectfully slink away?" he does, interestingly, admit that there may be "some genuinely profound and meaningful questions that are forever beyond the reach of science."[38] He posits quantum theory as one such entity; many Christians point to this very same theory in order to illustrate precisely that point.[39] Interestingly, Dawkins seems to retreat somewhat from scientism by conceding that "science's entitlement to advise us on moral values is problematic, to say the least."[40] But he then expresses immediate horror that his former colleague Gould could possibly have meant that *religion* had any right to offer any moral wisdom. Perish the thought!

These excerpts show the intrinsically aggressive and extremely hostile nature of Dawkins's atheism, directed not just at belief in religion, but even at tolerance of that belief. Dawkins mobilizes every single scientific argument that he can, including absolutely ridiculous notions like Bertrand Russell's "flying teapots" illustration (in which Russell argued that believing in God was as absurd as believing that a teapot revolved around the sun[41]). But Dawkins is not satisfied with making fun of religious belief; he wants to have no mercy on those who give any quarter to religion in scientific discussions. Thus Dawkins has a subsection of his long second chapter, "The God Hypothesis," called "The Neville Chamberlain School of Evolutionists."

As the title suggests, Dawkins seems to regard any scientific colleague, even if a proclaimed atheist, as a total appeaser of religionists if that person accedes in the slightest to the view that proponents of Darwinian evolution can also accept the validity of religious claims to truth. Dawkins attacks determined supporters of evolution in the evolution-creationism debate—people who logically would be regarded as being on Dawkins's side—because they make concessions to "sensible" or "mainstream" religious belief in their efforts to ensure that evolution continues to be taught in American schools. These advocates of evolution are willing to work with allies wherever they can find them, but this tactic enrages Dawkins, causing this reader to wonder if Dawkins can discuss any topic about which others might hold a differing view *without* getting angry. Once more, he fires a broadside at Michael Ruse, the philosopher of science mentioned in chapter one. Ruse had criticized Dawkins for rejecting any cooperation with the late Pope John Paul II, who made a speech in 1996 to the Pontifical Academy of Sciences that seemed to suggest that the theory of evolution did not violate or contradict Catholic theology. Ruse wrote that "Richard Dawkins's response was simply that the pope was a hypocrite, that he could not be genuine about science and that Dawkins himself simply preferred an honest fundamentalist."[42] Dawkins quotes Chicago geneticist Jerry Coyne's response to Ruse in which he asserts that Ruse "fails to grasp the real nature of the conflict," which, according to Coyne, is a "*real* war . . . between rationalism and superstition."[43]

The idea that science and religion are at war is by no means new; it is a dogma that emerged in the late nineteenth century. More importantly, it is a view that has been firmly rejected by the majority of scientists. Of course, Christian church authorities, both Catholic and Protestant, have at various times in history been suspicious of the implications of certain kinds of scientific discovery. But even Darwinism, though opposed by some Protestant groups, was warmly supported by others. As for Darwin himself, it is now acknowledged that his disappointment with Christianity stemmed not from his insights into evolutionary theory but from the personal tragedy experienced in his own family when his daughter Annie died at the age of ten. Chronic illnesses, which debilitated Darwin for months at a time and which today remain undiagnosed, were also a factor, because they made it difficult for him to reconcile a loving God with his experience of much suffering in his own life.

Darwin was not an atheist, though his views definitely changed over the course of his life. He had started out training to be a clergyman in the Anglican Church, but later in life said he was an agnostic. As he acknowledged in his autobiography, although he believed in a general idea of God ("When thus reflecting I feel compelled to look to a First Cause having an intelligent mind in some degree analogous to that of man; and I deserve to be called a Theist"[44]), this theistic view weakened over time, only occasionally boosted by doubts about whether the minds of Homo sapiens—who stand at the pinnacle of the human evolutionary process—could have emerged from the lower animals.[45] More strikingly, Darwin became aware that his ability to enjoy music, poetry, and art was becoming attenuated by the relentless need he felt to bring order to the vast volume of scientific data he was dealing with. This revealing passage from his autobiography poignantly demonstrates the price Darwin paid for his singular focus on science:

> But now for many years I cannot endure to read a line of poetry: I have tried lately to read Shakespeare, and found it so intolerably dull that it nauseated me. I have also almost lost any taste for pictures or music.—Music generally sets me thinking too energetically on what I have been at work on, instead of giving me pleasure. I retain some taste for fine scenery, but it does not cause me the exquisite delight which it formerly did. ... My mind seems to have become a kind of machine for grinding general laws out of large collections of facts. ...[46]

How profoundly sad. And yet how remarkably like another theoretician dedicated to "science," in this case "scientific socialism," as he would have called it—namely Vladimir Lenin, the Russian revolutionary and first Soviet head of state. Lenin wrote,

> I know nothing more beautiful than the Appassionata and I could listen to it every day. Wonderful, immortal music.

I always think, with perhaps a naive, childish pride, how can man create such wonders? But I cannot listen to music too often. It affects my nerves and makes me want to say sweet nothings and stroke the heads of men who live in a dirty hell and can still create such beauty. But these days you can't go around stroking people's heads lest your hand be bitten off. You have to smash them over the head—smash them without mercy—even though in theory we are against every form of oppression of mankind . . . ours is a hellish task.[47]

Albert Einstein is the ultimate scientist summoned by the Four Horsemen to be a witness in their case for atheism. It is certainly true, as Dawkins notes, that Einstein "did not believe in a personal God." Dawkins, however, can't stop at the facts of the case, that is, with the actual words of Einstein himself. He has to find some obtuse exponent of Christianity idiotically claiming Einstein as an ally, thus enabling Dawkins to "demonstrate" that such folly is typical of the religious attitude toward life. He brings up a letter written to Einstein by the president of a New Jersey historical association in which the writer admits great weakness in his own personal faith and expresses the hope that Einstein's skepticism toward a personal God has been a misquotation.

Dawkins cites the letter, from which he quotes a full sixteen lines, because, he says, it "damningly exposes the weakness of the religious mind."[48] This ploy is like quoting from the rantings of Osama bin Laden and saying that he is typical of all Muslims. Dawkins delivers what he thinks is the authoritative judgment on Einstein's religious views: He dismisses Einstein's statements that "God is subtle but he is not malicious" or "He does not play dice" or "Did God have a choice in creating the Universe?" and describes these comments as "pantheistic, not deistic, and certainly not theistic."[49]

Hitchens wraps himself in Einstein too, alleging that "he preserved what he could of ethical Judaism and rejected the barbaric mythology of the Pentateuch."[50] Hitchens doesn't explain what he means by "ethical Judaism," but since he is Jewish and an atheist, and yet considers himself a person of high moral principle, perhaps the term "ethical Judaism" means "all Jews who agree with Christopher Hitchens."

As for Harris, contemplation of Einstein's religious views moves him into a vaporous lyricism. "Einstein seemed to consider faith nothing more than a eunuch left to guard the harem while the intellect was away solving the problems of the world. By pretending that it could proceed without any epistemic aspirations whatsoever, Einstein robbed religion of the *truth* of its doctrine" (emphasis in the original).[51] Huh? What is it about Einstein that makes some atheists sound as if they have just come off an acid trip? Come to think of it, Harris started his search for—well, whatever it was a search for—after tripping out on ecstasy, so perhaps that explains his Einsteinisms.

Probably the most thoughtful and extended study of Einstein's views on religion has been laid out by Walter

Isaacson, former managing editor of *Time* magazine and author of several history books, including a highly praised biography of Benjamin Franklin. In 2007, Isaacson came out with a new biography on Einstein. Key excerpts from this book that deal with Einstein's "spiritual outlook"—to use as neutral a term as possible—were published in *Time*. From Isaacson's material, it is clear that, as Dawkins, Dennett, and Hitchens allege, Einstein did not believe in a personal God who intervenes in the universe and the affairs of humankind. And Hitchens is also correct that Einstein did share certain views with Baruch de Spinoza, the Dutch philosopher who is considered one of the great rationalists of the seventeenth century and whose ideas helped lay the foundation for the Enlightenment in the eighteenth century. But other than that, the evidence contradicts much of the portrait painted by Dawkins, Harris, and Hitchens. Einstein was absolutely not a pantheist, a label often applied to Spinoza, and Isaacson quotes Einstein saying so quite unequivocally,

> I'm not an atheist. I don't think I can call myself a pantheist. The problem involved is too vast for our limited minds. We are in the position of a little child entering a huge library filled with books in many languages. The child knows someone must have written those books. It does not know how. It does not understand the languages in which they are written. The child dimly suspects a mysterious order in the arrangement of the books but doesn't know

what it is. That, it seems to me, is the attitude of even the most intelligent human being toward God. We see the universe marvelously arranged and obeying certain laws but only dimly understand these laws.[52]

At a dinner party in Berlin (before Einstein emigrated from Germany to the United States), a guest who asserted that religion was mere superstition was silenced by his host, who noted that even Einstein was religious. "'It isn't possible!' the skeptical guest said, turning to Einstein to ask if he was, in fact, religious," Isaacson's account reports. "'Yes, you can call it that,' Einstein replied calmly. 'Try and penetrate with our limited means the secrets of nature and you will find that, behind all the discernible laws and connections, there remains something subtle, intangible and inexplicable. Veneration for this force beyond anything that we can comprehend is my religion. To that extent I am, in fact, religious.'"

If Einstein was angered by being described incorrectly as a follower of any organized religion, he was equally irritated at the atheists who claimed him as one of their own. "There are people who say there is no God," Isaacson reports Einstein telling a friend. "But what makes me really angry is that they quote me for support of such views." Isaacson further says that, unlike renowned atheists Sigmund Freud, Bertrand Russell, or George Bernard Shaw, Einstein never felt the urge to denigrate those who believed in God; instead, it was the atheists he tended to criticize. "What separates me from most so-called atheists is a feeling of utter humility toward the unattainable secrets of the harmony of the cosmos," he explained.

In fact, it wasn't simply that Einstein disagreed with the atheists; he really didn't like them. He once described "[t]he fanatical atheists" as being "like slaves who are still feeling the weight of their chains which they have thrown off after hard struggle. They are creatures who—in their grudge against traditional religion as the 'opium of the masses'—cannot hear the music of the spheres." While Einstein stayed away as far as he could from any Jewish synagogue or Christian church, he was surprisingly sympathetic to the personality of Jesus. "As a child I received instruction both in the Bible and in the Talmud," Isaacson quotes Einstein as saying. "I am a Jew, but I am enthralled by the luminous figure of the Nazarene." To another skeptical interlocutor who expressed amazement that Einstein believed Jesus even existed and who asked if it could be true, Einstein replied, "Unquestionably! No one can read the Gospels without feeling the actual presence of Jesus. His personality pulsates in every word. No myth is filled with such life."[53]

Einstein published his general theory of relativity in 1915. The following year, Bryn Mawr College sociologist James Leuba polled top scientists on whether they believed in God—defined as a personal God who communicates his thoughts to humanity. The results of this famous poll have been widely reported: roughly 40 percent believed in a personal God, and 40 percent did not. The remaining 20 percent were agnostic about the question. A 1996 poll asking the same question showed a slight increase in the percentage of atheists—to 45 percent—but exactly the same percentage of believers. Leuba in 1916 had predicted that, over time, there would be a significant reduction in the proportion of believers in a personal God among scientists. That didn't happen at all. Of course, there was a shifting of proportions between agnostics and atheists, with the latter gaining a 5 percent share, but that 40 percent constant of believers is remarkable.

As if to contradict further the Dawkins thesis that the study of the natural sciences is a superhighway to atheism, in 2006, the same year that the Four Horsemen started their gallop toward what they see as an apocalyptic battle between religious belief and atheism, two remarkable books written by scientists of profound religious conviction were published: Owen Gingerich's *God's Universe* and Francis Collins's *The Language of God: A Scientist Presents Evidence for Belief.*[54] Gingerich is professor emeritus of astronomy and the history of science at Harvard University. Collins is one of America's most distinguished geneticists and the director of the National Human Genome Leadership in Bethesda, Maryland, just outside Washington, D.C. Both are agnostics who converted to Christianity, and neither has jettisoned accepted scientific theories because of his faith.

In *God's Universe*, based on a series of lectures he gave at Harvard, Gingerich says that the universe was created "with intention and purpose, and that this belief does not interfere with the scientific enterprise." To show how the creator "fine-tuned" the universe, Gingerich points out that, at the time of the Big Bang, which cosmologists believe set in motion all subsequent developments in the universe, the balance between the outward energy of expansion and the gravitational forces trying to pull everything back together again had to be accurate to 10 to the power of 59. Another way of putting it is that the power of these two opposing forces had to be at a ratio of 1 to 1 followed by 59 zeroes (1:1000000000000000000000000000 00000000000000000000000000000000). It was exactly that, thus creating what Gingerich called a "congenial" environment in the universe for self-conscious life.

Collins has likewise assimilated his scientific professionalism with his personal faith and has no problem with the scientific theory of evolution, which he believes has been "theistic." In his view, the laws of nature that guided evolution were put into place by God. Collins says that the "central question" of his book is: "In this modern era of cosmology, evolution, and the human genome, is there still the possibility of a richly satisfying harmony between the scientific and spiritual worldviews? I answer with a resounding *yes*!" (emphasis in the original).[55]

Unlike Dawkins and Coyne, Gingerich sees no war between science and religion. In his view, not only is there no incompatibility between rigorous science and theistic belief, but a scientist's religious faith or lack thereof does not affect the quality of his scientific work. "One can *believe* that some of the evolutionary pathways are so intricate and so complex as to be hopelessly improbable by the rules of random chance" (emphasis in the original), Gingerich writes, "but if you do not believe in divine action, then you will simply have to say that random chance was extremely lucky, because the outcome is there to see. Either way, the scientist with theistic metaphysics will approach laboratory problems in much the same way as will his atheistic colleague across the hall."[56]

The British mathematician and metaphysician Alfred North Whitehead (1861–1947) made an interesting point about science in his book *Science and the Modern World*: "In the first place, there can be no living science unless there is a widespread instinctive conviction in the existence of an *Order of Things*, and, in particular, of an *Order of Nature*."[57] In contrast with some historians of science who believe that every useful development began sometime after the Reformation in 1517, Whitehead regarded the Middle Ages as the most important period leading up to the growth of modern science. He describes this period from approximately the fifth to the fifteenth centuries as "one long training of the intellect of Western Europe in the sense of order. . . . It was preeminently an epoch of orderly thought, rationalist through and through."[58] That rationalist thought developed from "the inexpugnable belief that every detailed occurrence can be correlated with its antecedents in a perfectly definite manner, exemplifying general principles," Whitehead explains. "Without this belief, the incredible labours of scientists would be without hope." He called this belief an "instinctive conviction." But how had it come about? Whitehead answered his own question thus: "It must come from the medieval insistence on the rationality of God, conceived as with the personal energy of Jehovah and with the rationality of a Greek philosopher. Every detail was supervised and ordered: the search into nature could only result in the vindication of the faith in rationality. Remember that I am not talking of the explicit beliefs of a few individuals. What I mean is the impress on the European mind arising from the unquestioned faith of centuries."[59]

"The unquestioned faith of centuries"? It suggests a conviction that was built upon the shoulders of men of faith (and some women) over an extended period of time until the conviction was indeed instinctive. And the conviction is this: that nature had order and it is the human challenge to uncover it. Thus, in Whitehead's view, science itself would have been impossible in its first confident steps into the unknown without habits of mind put in place by centuries of faith. Dawkins is more medieval than he knows. Hitchens is more monastic than he knows. And it is a good thing.

# Chapter Five

# THE

# PROBLEM OF

# WICKED ATHEISTS:

## STALIN, HITLER, MAO, AND POL POT

*"Every religious idea, every little god, even flirting with a little
god, is unutterable vileness . . . vileness of the most dangerous kind,
a plague of the most abominable kind. A million sins, filthy deeds,
acts of violence and physical plagues are much less dangerous."*
— Vladimir Lenin, 1913

Nothing puts the New Atheists more on the defensive
than people of faith who, having listened to the atheists'
inevitable laundry list of the wickedness perpetrated the world
over by adherents of religion, then chirp up with, "Well, what
about atheists such as Stalin, Hitler, Mao, and Pol Pot?" In
other words, haven't unapologetically atheistic regimes caused
far greater evil in the twentieth century than all the previous
religious wars put together? Daniel Dennett ignores this issue,
presumably because his attack on religion is predicated on the
allegation that religious belief is some sort of evolutionary
aberration, a virus, or a case of odd memes popping up here

and there. In spite of being a philosopher, he's all science. But Richard Dawkins tackles it head-on. "The question comes up," he writes wearily, displaying the annoyance of a third-grade teacher asked yet again how to spell *recess*, "after just about every public lecture I ever give on the subject of religion, and in most of my radio interviews as well."[1]

"What matters is not whether Hitler and Stalin were atheists," Dawkins continues, framing the issue to his liking, "but whether atheism systematically *influences* people to do bad things. There is not the smallest evidence that it does" (emphasis in the original).[2] Dawkins does admit that the ruthless Soviet dictator Joseph Stalin was an atheist, but is ambivalent about whether Nazi dictator and Holocaust instigator Adolf Hitler was. With commendable honesty, he acknowledges that in Hitler's case, the evidence is open to interpretation. He cites the fact that Hitler never formally renounced his childhood Catholicism and that, at different points in his life, he did express himself in terms suggestive of some religious belief. Dawkins quotes Hitler deputy Rudolf Hess (1894–1987) saying in a 1920 conversation with the prime minister of Bavaria that Hitler was "a good Catholic." More pertinently, Dawkins quotes Hitler in 1933, after he had risen to power in Germany, as saying that the Nazis had undertaken a fight against atheism, and indeed, had "stamped it out."[3] He also quotes Hitler saying in his autobiography *Mein Kampf* that he was "acting in accordance with the will of the Almighty Creator: *by defending myself against the Jew, I am fighting for the work of the Lord*" (emphasis in the original).[4] But Dawkins does again display some commendable intellectual honesty in also citing a well-known source for assessing Hitler's personal philosophy, the *Table Talk* transcripts of Hitler's mealtime musings, as recorded by powerful Hitler aide Martin Bormann. These indicate, as we shall see, that Hitler's devotion to the Catholic Church was purely formal and that he departed decisively from Catholic teaching or any Christian moral conviction when it came to treatment of people who were ethnically or philosophically different from the Nazis.

Sam Harris, like many secular or atheistic Jews, wishes to portray Hitler as unequivocally Christian and his genocide against the Jewish people as merely continuing—*a little more thoroughly perhaps*—a legacy of German anti-Semitism that goes back to Martin Luther, founder of Protestantism in 1546, and beyond. When it comes to Mao Tse-tung, Hitler, and Stalin and the charge that they are heinous examples of militant atheism in power, Harris tries to perform a magician's trick in their defense by arguing that "while it is true that such men are sometimes enemies of organized religion, they are never especially rational."[5] In other words, since they were somehow delusional, they weren't, well, *regular* atheists. Harris goes on to say that "the problem with such tyrants is not that they reject the dogma of religion, but that they embrace other life-destroying myths."[6]

But that is *precisely* the point. As we shall see, atheism opens the door to life-destroying myths in a way that caused more misery in the twentieth century than any other single fundamental worldview. Does that mean that all atheists are deluded into following benighted ideologies and lunatic notions of class and race? Of course not. Many, if not most, atheists are patriotic, honest, hardworking, and charitable members of their society. That is not in question. What is in question is whether atheism is, on balance, good or not good once it has been adopted as the dominant philosophy for matters related to ethics and morality.

A self-confessed "unrepentant atheist," former member of Parliament, and longtime socialist, Roy Hattersley, looked at this question the other way around in a 2005 column in Britain's *The Guardian* with the subheading, "We atheists have to accept that most believers are better human beings." He observed that "almost all" the aid groups that stayed on in Hurricane Katrina–ravaged parts of New Orleans long after the first wave of relief workers had left "have a religious origin and character," whereas, "notable by their absence are teams from rationalist societies, free thinkers' clubs and atheists' associations—the sort of people who not only scoff at religion's intellectual absurdity but also regard it as a positive force for evil." From his observations not just of Salvation Army workers and other Christians in New Orleans but also in his constituency when he was in politics, Hattersley conceded, "The only possible conclusion is that faith comes with a packet of moral imperatives that, while they do not condition the attitude of all believers, influence enough of them to make them morally superior to atheists like me. The truth may make us free. But it has not made us as admirable as the average captain in the Salvation Army."[7]

Of the Four Horsemen, Christopher Hitchens at least admits that "secular totalitarianism has actually provided us with the *summa* of human evil."[8] Hitchens also has a much more accurate assessment of Nazism than Harris has. He describes it as "a quasi-pagan phenomenon which in the long run sought to replace Christianity with pseudo-Nordic blood rites and sinister race myths, based upon the fantasy of Aryan superiority." Hitchens, somewhat contradictorily (because his entire book tries to make the case that *nothing is ever good in any religion*), credits the German church with having publicly denounced one of Hitler's evil crimes—"an exterminationist attitude to the unwell, the unfit, and the insane"—even before Hitler began systematically to deal with the Jews.[9] But, in typical Hitchens fashion, he immediately tries to put the blame for Hitler's wicked crimes not on the evil secular dictator himself but back on religious believers, particularly those in the Roman Catholic Church, for essentially having encouraged his coming to power in the first place. Finally, Hitchens blames *religion* for the monstrosities of Stalin's and Mao's antireligious regimes because "the religious impulse—the need to worship—can take even more monstrous forms if it is suppressed."[10] In other words, religion is essentially to blame for the way it has been thoroughly and cruelly suppressed in the hands of atheism. You can't win with Hitchens; if a churchgoer is murdered by his neighbor, Hitchens would say it was probably because the neighbor was constantly annoyed by the victim's church attendance, which reminded the neighbor that he himself might end up in hell.

Hitchens goes wildly offtrack on North Korea, which he visited in 2000 (I was there in 1983), by describing it as "not so much an extreme form of Communism—the term is hardly mentioned amid the storms of ecstatic dedication—as a debased yet refined form of Confucianism and ancestor worship."[11] (He also goes off on one of his bizarre "mammal" riffs, referring to "the ludicrous mammal Kim Il Sung and his pathetic mammal son, Kim Jong Il"). The Confucian simile is absurd, and Hitchens reveals his ignorance of this Chinese philosophy, which has an inbuilt, self-correcting mechanism against the very kind of megalomania exhibited by Kim Il Sung and perpetuated by his son. Although ancient Chinese history has its share of evil emperors who ruled with excessive and wanton cruelty, nothing in the entire history of Confucianism even approaches the totalitarian evil of North Korea's Orwellian, insane society. That's because Confucianism extols moderation, venerates the benevolent ruler governing a harmonious society, and gives the people the right to revolt against an evil regime. In fact, quite contrary to Hitchens's thesis that "religion poisons everything," some students of Chinese history have noted a correlation between the wickedness of an emperor's rule and his abandonment of ancient Chinese religious practices, a trend that leads eventually to the downfall of the dynasty.[12] The rise and fall of dynasties was governed by "the mandate of Heaven," that is, the concept that the right to rule was granted by God, and this cycle was repeated again and again throughout China's four-thousand-year history.[13] As for the comparison with North Korea, let Hitchens come up with even one example of the paranoia, xenophobic hatred of outsiders, and almost unimaginable daily cruelty in the two millennia or so of Confucianism's predominance in the history of China comparable to the wickedness perpetrated in North Korea. Of course, he can't.

The point that needs to be made about the role of atheism in the depravities of twentieth-century secular totalitarian dictatorships is this: Simply put, atheism sets mankind at the very center of the universe. That is, atheism makes the assumption that there is no authority for rightness or wrongness of human behavior outside of human beings themselves. This is an assumption with which all the Four Horsemen and indeed all atheists would surely agree. Indeed, atheists in general are on record as saying that in matters of human behavior, there are no absolutes of right or wrong at all, no good or evil, other than, at best, a consensus of what is good or bad for a particular society at a particular time.[14] Atheists are quick to point out that, even with such absolutes in place, religious people often have transgressed clearly known moral restrictions. That is true, of course. But for religious people, the moral restrictions on acceptable behavior are acknowledged and can be openly examined and discussed. People of faith who transgress them can be—and are—held accountable, not only by those who subscribe to the same faith but even by atheists, as well as by people of other faiths. For atheists, who have no consensus on absolutes outside of themselves and their own community, the line separating good from evil is potentially in a state of constant flux.

More important, what the Four Horsemen all ignore is the fact that the twentieth-century ideologies that produced the greatest totalitarian evils, communism and Nazism, both grew out of a sustained philosophical rebellion against religious faith—in essence, atheism. That philosophical rebellion was birthed in the eighteenth-century French Enlightenment and first gained expression in political life during the 1789–1799 French Revolution; it attained its apotheosis in the Bolshevik regime that came to rule Russia after October 1917. When French Enlightenment writer and philosopher Voltaire asserted in 1768, "If God did not exist, it would be necessary to invent him,"[15] he was expressing deist, not atheist, beliefs. But by the time the French Revolution approached the paroxysm of the Reign of Terror in 1793, atheism was in conflict with deism. Dechristianization had become the policy of the revolutionary regime, leading to decrees that priests and those who harbored them could be killed on sight. In the wholesale bloodletting of the ten-month Reign of Terror, 18,500 to 40,000 French men and women were executed, including thousands of priests and their protectors.

By then, other developments were already unfolding that would have a far more profound impact on the course of world history than the terrifying violence of the French Revolution. In Germany, a storm of assaults on the veracity and historicity of the Bible had been raging in German universities in the second half of the eighteenth century. Out of that maelstrom—essentially predicated on a refusal to believe that anything biblical was supernatural in origin—a philosopher emerged whose impact and long-term influence on European thinking was incalculable. He was Friedrich Hegel (1770–1831), and he left an indelible mark on all the major thinkers and writers of the remainder of the nineteenth century.[16] In fact, in his 1795 work, "The Life of Jesus," he puts into Christ's mouth these words: "Act on the maxim which you can at the same time will to be a universal law among men. This is the fundamental law of morality—the content of all legislation and of the sacred books of all nations."[17] This idea comes straight from Immanuel Kant (1724–1804), the German philosopher and writer who not only had enormous influence on Hegel but who is also considered the most influential thinker of modern Europe, and whom Dawkins quotes with approval.[18]

Hegel's most radical followers were known in the 1830s and 1840s as the "Young Hegelians," and it was their writings that changed beyond recognition the way the European intelligentsia viewed religion. In the 1740s, a handful of writers had certainly begun to challenge orthodox Christianity, but most educated people in the West still believed it to be true in most respects. One hundred years later, it had been dethroned—not among ordinary citizens of Europe and North America, but certainly among identifiable leaders of trends in thought and philosophy. Out of this intellectual turmoil of the 1840s emerged the looming figure of Karl Marx (1818–1883), whose seminal call to revolution, *The Communist Manifesto*, was written in 1848. But before Marx became really well known, the most important of the Young Hegelians was Ludwig Feuerbach, whose 1841 book, *The Essence of Christianity*, had absolutely enormous influence on several generations of German and Russian intellectuals. It was first translated into English in 1854 by the British novelist George Eliot, who was called a freethinker in those days (essentially an agnostic). Feuerbach's insight was that religion, and Christianity in particular, was entirely man-made. Hitchens makes the same assertion several times in *God Is Not Great*, saying that the "most radical" and at the same time "most devastating" criticism of religion is that "religion is man-made."[19] There's nothing original in Hitchens; Feuerbach actually came up with the idea first, writing, "The fundamental dogmas of Christianity are realized wishes of the heart; the essence of Christianity is the essence of human feeling."[20] He added:

> The necessary turning-point of history is therefore the open confession, that the consciousness of God is nothing else than the consciousness of the species . . . that there is no other essence which man can think, dream of, imagine, feel, believe in, wish for, love and adore as the *absolute*, than the essence of human nature itself. (emphasis in the original)[21]

German-Jewish philosopher Moses Hess (1812–1879), an early socialist as well as a Zionist, was the fellow Jew who introduced the young Karl Marx to the notion of communism in the sphere of economics. Hess wrote to a friend in September 1841 that Marx would "give the *coup de grace* to medieval religion and politics."[22] Arnold Ruge, a contemporary of Marx who was also a Young Hegelian, wrote to a friend in the same month that Feuerbach and several others, including rabidly anti-Christian German theology professor Bruno Bauer, "are proclaiming or have already proclaimed the *Montagne*, and raised up the flag of Atheism and Human mortality. God, religion, immortality are deposed and a philosophical republic proclaimed, with men as Gods."[23] This declaration that men had taken over from the gods was a trifle premature, although Marx was indeed that very year planning to bring out a periodical called *Archiv der Atheismus* (*Atheist Archive*). Also that same year, Marx had completed his doctoral dissertation *The Difference between the Democritean and Epicurean Philosophy of Nature*. These bellicose words appear in its preface: "Philosophy makes no secret of it. The proclamation of Prometheus: 'In a word, I detest all gods,' is its own confession, its own aphorism against all heavenly and earthly gods who do not acknowledge human self-consciousness as the highest divinity. It will have none other beside."[24] (In his preface, Marx uses the original Greek in quoting Prometheus, the character in Greek mythology who stole fire from the gods and brought it to humans, but I provided the English translation directly in quoting his text.)

Two years later, Marx introduced into the world one of his most frequently quoted (and misquoted) comments on religion—his "opium of the people" observation—in the *Contribution to the Critique of Hegel's Philosophy of Law*. Because the passage is such an important part of the Marxist and atheist scriptural canon—Hitchens, a former Marxist and Trotskyist, of course quotes it—we will look here at the full passage rather than just the single sentence that is commonly quoted.

> For Germany, *the criticism of religion* has been essentially completed, and the criticism of religion is the prerequisite of all criticism. . . .
>
> The foundation of irreligious criticism is: *Man makes religion*, religion does not make man. . . . The struggle against religion is therefore indirectly the struggle *against that world* whose spiritual *aroma* is religion.
>
> . . . Religion is the sigh of the oppressed creature, the heart of a heartless world, and the soul of soulless conditions. It is the *opium* of the people.
>
> . . . The criticism of religion is, therefore, *in embryo, the criticism of that vale of tears* of which religion is the *halo*. (emphasis in the original)[25]

In other words, the reason Marx and other Young Hegelians were waging such an energetic assault upon religious belief was to provide irrefutable philosophical reasoning for an assault upon the political and economic realities of life that caused people to inhabit "the vale of tears." In marshaling all forces of the intellect for that assault, Marx emphasized, criticism of religion was "the prerequisite of all criticism."

Marx died in 1883, and his collaborator, Friedrich Engels, in 1895. Before his death, each man attempted to organize groups of followers of "scientific socialism," Marx's supposed lifelong discovery of the laws of history. In Western Europe, they achieved decidedly mixed success. Marxist revolutionism was being overtaken by socialist parliamentarism. For example, in Europe's most economically industrialized nation—Britain—workers were gravitating to the view that they could gain political power, and thus improve their own conditions, more effectively by working from within the system rather than by trying to overturn it wholesale. The year 1900 saw the founding, for example, of the British Labour Party, which for years proclaimed socialism as its goal. Many of Labour's early leaders were not atheists at all but adherents of Christian socialism; for example, James Keir Hardie (1856–1915), one of the first two Labour Party MPs, was a convert from atheism to Christianity and remained a devout believer throughout his life. His Christian beliefs strongly influenced his politics, and he also served as a lay preacher in his church.

This strong linkage between politics and religion in the late nineteenth century was having a profound social impact, one that deeply troubled Marx and Engels. The following story illustrates just how it incensed them. While playing a well-known Victorian parlor game with Karl Marx's daughter, Engels answered with a single word a "Confessions" question ("What is your favorite motto?" "What is your favorite color?" etc.) that asked whom he most hated in life. "Spurgeon" was Engels's curt, one-word answer, referring to English Baptist evangelist Charles Spurgeon (1834–1892), whose sermons in the 1850s to the 1880s drew as many as twenty thousand people, many of them working-class folk. Why did Engels hate him so? Because Spurgeon was diverting England's urban working class away from atheist revolutionary socialism to Christian parliamentary reformism. Indeed, the phenomenon of evangelistic Christian work among England's working class was so widespread that Karl Marx noticed it while vacationing in the English seaside county of Sussex in 1874. In a letter to Engels, Marx wrote, "Our landlord is a scripture reader for the poor and his theological library, about two dozen volumes, decorates our sitting room. Though he belongs to the Church of England, I found Spurgeon's sermons there. In Sandown, where I took a hot bath . . . you can't take a single step without seeing pious meetings advertised."

In one part of Europe, however, the soil was richly accepting of both Marxist socialism and the radical atheism that went with it. Russia, a country whose Orthodox Christianity had inoculated it against the religious, cultural, and political ferment of the Protestant Reformation, was still ruled by an autocratic monarch presiding over a social system characterized by serfdom, a system in which peasant tenants were "owned" by the landed nobility and had no individual rights whatsoever. Russia had certainly experienced a touch of the European Enlightenment, but the ruling tsar at the time, Catherine the Great (1729–1796), though she corresponded warmly with Voltaire and loved to think of herself as "the Enlightened monarch," made sure that intellectual dissent in Russia was allowed to pose no threat whatsoever to existing social and economic conditions.

After the deaths of Catherine and her successors, Russian intellectuals and champions of radical social change embraced the hatred for religion that was to characterize them for most of the period from the 1860s to the 1917 Bolshevik Revolution. "The intelligentsia" was the term used to refer to any Russian with more than secondary education who had an interest in ideas, and it continues even today to denote intellectuals who see themselves collectively as the vanguard of thought in any society. In Russia, the intelligentsia had been politically liberal in the 1840s, supportive of reform but not of revolution. Two decades later, though, to be a member of the intelligentsia was almost by definition to be an atheist and a socialist, committed to the most radical change possible, preferably through revolution. Typical of the revolutionaries who emerged from that milieu was Mikhail Bakunin (1814–1876), who influenced several of Russia's most radical revolutionaries. In his rage against God, however, he went beyond most of them, declaring, for instance, "I reverse the phrase of Voltaire and say that, *if God really existed, it would be necessary to abolish him*" (emphasis in the original).[26]

Vladimir Lenin (1870–1924), the first leader of any state

that openly espoused atheism as its philosophical worldview, which Russia did after the November 7, 1917, Bolshevik Revolution, was born too late to have known Bakunin. But in his adolescence and young manhood, he was profoundly influenced by many young radicals who had themselves been influenced by Bakunin. Lenin was sympathetic to all the atheist ideas that originated from the writings of the Young Hegelians even before he decided that Marxism offered the keys to changing Russia and the world, and in the 1890s, while still in his twenties, he adopted Marxism as his worldview. Once he had become the acknowledged leader of the Bolsheviks—that is, of the radical section of the opposition political party, the Russian Social-Democratic Labour Party—in 1902, Lenin never wavered from an attitude of what seemed to be permanent rage at God, or against any theistic ideas. In a famous letter to the Russian writer Maxim Gorky in 1913, Lenin was venomously explicit about his atheist views.

> Every religious idea, every little god, even flirting with a little god, is unutterable vileness . . . vileness of the most dangerous kind, a plague of the most abominable kind. A million sins, filthy deeds, acts of violence and physical plagues are much less dangerous than the subtle, spiritual idea of a god dressed up in the smartest intellectual costumes. A Catholic priest who seduces young girls . . . is far less dangerous for 'democracy' than a priest without a cassock, a priest without crude religion, a principled and

democratic priest who advocates the construction and creation of a little god.[27]

Lenin's outlook of quite open rage and hatred set the stage for all of the subsequent acts of violence and cruelty that the Soviet state committed against religious believers for nearly a full century, from 1917 until the collapse of communism in 1991. Lenin, in fact, seemed to think that religion was a "plague"—this notion was *not* invented by Dawkins—and that it could only be removed from the human brain by "disinfection" in the form of mockery and insults. He set about in quick order to try to blot out all religious influence and activity. The Bolsheviks' very first decree, just one day after seizing power in Petrograd (later called Leningrad, and now renamed St. Petersburg), was the Decree on Land, written by Lenin himself, ordering the confiscation of all ecclesiastical and monastic lands. A little over a month later, another decree deprived the Orthodox church of all its property. One week after that, still in December 1917, all the monasteries were closed down. A few days later, the Christian marriage ceremony was replaced by a civil rite.

In February 1918, Lenin promulgated a decree separating church from state. Americans might say, "Very good, we believe in that." But what Lenin really had in mind for religion was made abundantly clear in the section dealing with freedom of conscience. This was nothing like the First Amendment to the U.S. Constitution, which says "Congress shall make no law respecting the establishment of a religion, or preventing the free exercise thereof." Rather, as Lenin explained it, "After the implementation of the separation of church from state and school from church have taken effect, it is essential to strive for the separation of the people from religion and the church."[28] The decree concludes with the words "Remember that the struggle against religions is a struggle for socialism!"[29]

Already, thousands of priests, pious laypeople, monks, nuns, and others were being rounded up and sent off to the *gulag*—the Soviet Union's widespread system of forced-labor camps—which, as Russian writer and political dissident Aleksandr Solzhenitsyn makes clear in *The Gulag Archipelago*, Lenin was firmly putting into place long before Stalin came to power.[30] Thousands of others were simply executed by shooting. Many of those arrested were sent to the famous Solovetsky Monastery, in the far north of Russia, which in 1921 was turned into one of the very earliest models of the Soviet labor camp system. As happened under the rule of every single atheist regime henceforth, the grounds for arresting people of faith seldom were what they themselves believed privately; rather, they were arrested on grounds of what they were teaching to their children and others. According to Solzhenitsyn in *The Gulag Archipelago*, under the Soviet penal code Article 58-10, which dealt with "counter-revolutionary agitation and propaganda" and went into effect in 1927, teaching a child about religious belief was a crime, and the sentence for instructing a son or daughter in the Lord's Prayer, for example, was ten years in the *gulag*.[31] A Russian Christian poet, Tanya Khodkevich, was sentenced to ten years in prison for writing these words:

> You can pray *freely*,
> But just so God alone can hear. (emphasis in the original)[32]

The Bolsheviks, who in 1918 reorganized themselves into the Communist Party, issued a series of decrees from the early days of the revolution onward that progressively restricted religious rights. As often as possible, they chose to insult people of faith deliberately. In September 1921, Lenin asked the Politburo to prohibit the sale of "pornography and books with religious content" and for such material to be treated as "wastepaper" and turned over to the proper authorities.[33] (The Chinese Communists used exactly the same tactic six decades later during the 1983–1984 campaign against "spiritual pollution" with an editorial in the *People's Daily*, the Communist Party mouthpiece, denouncing "pornography and religion.") In Lenin's Russia, show trials against religious figures began the following year, with the gentle Metropolitan Veniamin of Petrograd, one of the highest hierarchs of the Russian Orthodox Church, displaying great dignity when he was arrested for resisting the confiscation of sacred church artifacts by the state and charged with inciting worshippers against the Soviet government. He was found guilty and executed by shooting, one of the first of thousands, perhaps hundreds of thousands, of clerics,

Christian believers from all denominations, and devoted followers of other religions who were put to death in the atheist Soviet state's gigantic execution machine.

Lenin would not let up on religion, even when it was quite obvious that religious opposition in no way posed any kind of threat to his regime. In an October 1921 editorial in *Pravda*, the Communist Party mouthpiece, he declared, "We have fought and are fighting religion in earnest."[34] A veritable witches' glee of atheistic exuberance in attacking religion, especially Christianity, broke out in the Soviet Union in the 1920s. "Anti-God" exhibits went up all over the country, and the tombs of venerated saints were exhumed in order to show that their purportedly miracle-producing remains had actually rotted away rather than being miraculously preserved, as some Orthodox Church believers held. In 1922, a new newspaper was founded, *Bezbozhnik* (*The Godless*), and became *The League of the Godless* in 1925. That year, another antireligious publication, *Antireligioznik* (*The Anti-Religionist*), was founded. Both went to almost ludicrous lengths to express rage against the deity. "The belief in, and the reliance upon God, whoever he is—whether Jewish, Moslem, Christian or Buddhist—weakens the will to struggle, to reorganization of the world," read one editorial.[35]

The Soviet government newspaper, *Izvestiia*, made clear in a January 1923 editorial that the aim of the Soviet leadership's antireligious policy was not to purify or reform religion—say, to make its practitioners repent for having supposedly duped and oppressed the people—but to destroy it. "Our aim," said the editorial, "is not to 'renovate' the church, but to abolish it, to eradicate all religion. That aim can be achieved only when society is organized upon communist principles. . . . So far, we have had little time to pay serious attention to religious prejudices. We were confronted with things much more urgent and important. But now the time has changed and soon all this filthy idolatry will be swept away."[36]

The Soviet media at the time called the antireligious activities of the 1920s "the assault on heaven"—a rather nonsensical idea since, according to Marxism-Leninism, heaven doesn't even exist, so how can it be assaulted? In Paris, the exiled Russian intellectual Peter Struve, a materialist and Marxist in the 1890s who turned to Christianity in reaction to what he saw as the ugliness in personal and political behavior of unchecked atheism, was astonished and saddened by what was happening. The entire Soviet campaign, he said, was "a war against God and faith" carried out in the name of a "deified humanity." Indeed it was. The Soviet experience thoroughly demonstrates that if God is eliminated from public life, a much worse deity inevitably is erected in his place.

In fact, Lenin made abundantly plain that he not only did not believe in God, he disbelieved in morality itself. In this, he and Sam Harris disagree; Harris believes that it is possible in an atheist world to have "moral" judgments without defining what constitutes "morality." Lenin, however, speaking to the Communist Youth League in 1920, said:

In what sense do we reject ethics, reject morality?

In the sense given to it by the bourgeoisie, who based ethics on God's commandments . . .

We say that our morality is entirely subordinated to the interests of the proletariat's class struggle. Our morality stems from the interests of the class struggle of the proletariat.[37]

In essence, this is gangster ethics, the morality of the mafia guiding the policies of national government. It also happens to be determinedly atheist.

The campaigns initiated directly by Lenin or implemented during his 1917–1924 leadership of the Soviet Union were only the beginning of a purgatory of horrors inflicted by the regime on religious believers, and indeed on anyone who did not absorb wholesale the new partyspeak and the official atheism. Lenin's death in 1924 was followed by a political interregnum during which Lenin's successors, including Stalin, Leon Trotsky, Comintern head Grigory Zinoviev, Politburo chairman Lev Kamenev, and *Pravda* editor Nikolai Bukharin maneuvered for power. By 1927, Stalin had emerged the victor (exiling Trotsky, then later having him murdered in exile in Mexico), and shortly thereafter he began planning a dramatic radicalization of Soviet domestic policies.

In May 1929, the Soviet Constitution's language on religious freedom was changed to abolish the previous guarantee of freedom to propagate the faith (this freedom did not apply to the proselytizing of children) and to add "the right of professing a religion and of anti-religious propaganda." Huge numbers of churches were closed, sacred icons seized and then sold to foreign buyers for hard currency, priceless wall murals desecrated and destroyed, and the last remaining monasteries and convents shut down. In January 1930, a Soviet organization called the League of Militant Godless claimed to have two million members. The following year, 3,200 "godless shock brigades" were reported to be operating in the Soviet Union, and the wholesale destruction of church buildings all across Russia began by the thousands.

Richard Dawkins makes the very unlearned assertion on page 249 of *The God Delusion* that no "atheist in the world would bulldoze Mecca—or Chartres, York Minster or Notre Dame . . . etc., etc.," referring respectively to Islam's holiest city, the French Cathedral of Our Lady of Chartres (considered to be one of the finest examples of Gothic architecture), northern Europe's largest Gothic cathedral located in the northern English city of York, and Paris's famed Roman Catholic cathedral, as well as mentioning important structures in other religions, including Buddhism. A more careful student of history than Dawkins would have known, however, that an atheist did indeed do just that. That person was Joseph Stalin. In December 1931, he ordered the largest Russian Orthodox church in Moscow (and the tallest Eastern Orthodox church in the world), the Cathedral of Christ the Savior, dynamited in broad daylight as thousands of stupefied Russian Christians watched in horror. The destruction was not simply part of Stalin's continuing campaign to humiliate Christian believers; he had grandiose plans for a gigantic structure in its place. He wanted to construct on the site a gargantuan skyscraper to the glory of communism. It was to be called "The Palace of the Soviets," and when completed, was to be taller than the newly built Empire State Building and capped with a 300-foot-tall statue of Lenin blessing mankind.

Well, everyone knows what happens to even the best-laid plans. No sooner had construction started on the site of the demolished cathedral (it took an entire year just to remove the rubble) than streams of water flowing in underground rivulets from the Moscow River began to seep into the foundations of what was to be "The Palace of the Soviets" as they were being laid. Engineers battled the pesky subterranean flow but never succeeded in constructing anything taller than the metal framework of the first few stories. (Of course, no one considered praying for a solution.) The rusting framework was standing in silent reproach to Stalin's grandiose scheme a decade later when the Germans invaded the Soviet Union in June 1941. At this point, Stalin decided that the metal framework was urgently needed for war production and stopped the project. After the war, the cavernous foundations for the promised Palace were turned into the world's largest open-air swimming pool, heated for use in winter.[38]

In the thirteen years beginning in 1927, when Stalin first established his control over the Soviet Union, the number of functioning churches in Russia fell from more than 25,000 to fewer than 500. In the same period, some 130,000 Orthodox priests were arrested, of whom an estimated 95,000 were executed. Unknown thousands more perished namelessly in the *gulag*. No doubt many had been given ten-year sentences for having instructed their own children in the faith. Revealingly, the 1937 census was said to have uncovered the fact that, despite nearly two decades of relentless atheistic propaganda, 40 percent of the entire Soviet population still reported belief in God.[39] This statistic can only be reported as rumor because the census results were never published, and furthermore, ranking officials of the census bureau were sent to the *gulag* because the census data also showed a disastrous decline in the population numbers—which is what happens when you deliberately starve people to death, as was done to approximately 15 million rich peasants, or *kulaks*.

It is well known, of course, that Stalin dramatically reversed his antireligious policy once Hitler invaded the Soviet Union in 1941. The Russian Orthodox Church had traditionally identified itself with Russian patriotism, and indeed the Cathedral of Christ the Savior that Stalin dynamited in 1931 had been constructed in the nineteenth century in thanksgiving to God for Russia's victory over Napoleon. To defeat the Germans, Stalin needed moral help from the very Christians that Soviet atheist propagandists had spent some twenty years instructing people how to mock and ridicule. Thousands of churches were reopened, and the Moscow Theological Academy and

Seminary, which the Bolsheviks had closed in 1918, was allowed to again hold classes. This improved state of affairs for Russia's Christians—the various Protestant denominations were included in the resumed tolerance—lasted until 1959, when Stalin successor Nikita Khrushchev initiated a sustained propaganda and administrative attack once more on religion in the Soviet Union. Khrushchev ordered the closure of some 12,000 churches and stepped up once again an atheist propaganda campaign. By 1985, which marked the end of the era of Khrushchev and his successor, Leonid Brezhnev, only about 7,000 functioning churches existed in the entire 8.6-million-square-mile expanse of the Soviet Union.

Yet this prolonged and concentrated attempt to purge the Soviet Union of all religious belief didn't simply backfire, it spawned a new form of worship: a cult with Lenin as a new Communist deity. The slogan "Lenin lived, Lenin lives, Lenin will live" was tirelessly repeated in the Soviet Union even into the 1980s. The lyrics of a popular song went, "Lenin lives in my heart," as though by altering the words of a powerful and foundational Christian idea ("Christ lives in my heart"), the Soviet regime could appropriate the devotion of all Christians throughout history for the founder of their faith, Jesus Christ.

Freudian observers of this phenomenon, of this need in all societies for godlike figures to revere, would say that it is an expression of the universal human longing for a father figure. Others would argue that in hitherto Christian-majority cultures, it is only natural for new regimes coming to power to attempt to replicate the focus of worship previously represented by God and Jesus Christ. This was certainly the case in the Soviet Union where an image of Stalin as an all-wise, all-knowing, all-but-infallible ruler was projected to the Soviet people by Communist Party propagandists.

Yet how should the cultivation of a savior-like cult be explained in a society which, before the communist revolution, was not Christian at all, or at least one in which Christians were a small minority? This is the question that immediately arises with regard to the most extreme and absurd political personality cult in the world, indeed probably of all time: North Korea's Communist leader Kim Il Sung (1912–1994). Kim, a major in the Soviet army that swept into Korea after World War II to accept the Japanese surrender in 1945, literally rode into power atop a Soviet tank. He then quickly secured his own political dynasty by ruthlessly purging any political figures who appeared to contradict him or rival him. He was prime minister from 1948 to 1972, whereupon he became president.

The official titles, though, were less important than the way he determinedly contrived to be regarded—even worshipped— as a deity. Operas were written with words like "He is our savior." Statues of him, with arm extended Lenin-style, are today found throughout North Korea and given the reverence due to religious shrines; visitors to North Korea are encouraged, indeed are expected, to leave a bouquet of flowers at these statues. Even portraits of Kim, which are required to be hung in all public buildings, have to be handled with the same reverence that in the past would have been accorded to religious icons. Children are taught to thank Kim Il Sung for all blessings, and all North Koreans wear buttons bearing his portrait on their lapels. Just in case the point still isn't abundantly clear, the constitution has declared Kim Il Sung to be the "Eternal President" of North Korea, even though he did actually die back in 1994. While alive, Kim was referred to as the "Great Leader," and his son, who now rules North Korea, as the "Dear Leader." Kim Jong Il, the son, has graduated to "Great Leader" status since taking over from his father, and he has shown no sign whatsoever of lessening the idolatry he inherited from his father.

What accounts for this almost psychopathic need to acquire the aura of divinity? In North Korea's case, the answer is complex, because Pyongyang before World War II had such a vibrant and large Christian community that it was known as "the Jerusalem of Asia." (The late Ruth Graham, wife of evangelist Billy Graham and daughter of medical missionaries to China, went to school in Pyongyang when she was in her late teens.) According to some reports, Kim himself actually attended a Christian school for a while, his parents were active Christian believers, and his grandfather was a minister. With such a background, he would certainly be familiar with the words of praise sung by Christians to their Savior. The larger explanation for the cult of divinity is that the more wicked the acts of a tyrant are, the more his claimed legitimacy needs to be raised so high that it is quite above human accountability.

In this regard, Kim Il Sung is no exception: There are a number of legends attributing supernatural powers to him.

All sensible atheists in the West, of course, abhor the human rights abuses that have characterized North Korea since its founding and the incredible cruelty of the regime, relentlessly determined to stay in power. What many are reluctant to admit, however, is this strikingly obvious quandary: If you declare humanity to be the only ultimate value in the world, from whence do you derive the authority to pronounce moral judgment on regimes that themselves do not recognize any authority higher than humanity? Does that authority come from a *New York Times* poll of college professors on the question of what ought to be deemed "immoral" or "unethical"? Or from a consensus of atheists meeting in conference to discuss political wickedness? "Humanity," in the sense of "compassion" and "respect for human dignity," is an attractive virtue, acknowledged by most people of faith—and I assume by most atheists as well—to characterize people regardless of their faith or non-faith positions. But it's hardly a rallying cry for great courage or moral determination to resist evil. Instinctively, intuitively, people seem to recognize that something more is needed.

Before leaving communist atheism and going on to Hitler, mention must be made of China, whose regime when led by Communist leader Chairman Mao Tse-tung imposed atheist education in all schools and universities and launched frequent campaigns viciously targeted at religious believers of all faiths. When it took power in China in 1949 after winning a protracted civil war, the Communist Party recognized five official religions: Buddhism, Daoism (China's only indigenous belief system), Islam, Catholicism, and Protestantism. The designation of Catholicism as a separate "religion" rather than as falling under the umbrella of Christianity was a matter of administrative convenience for the Party, not a result of confusion over Christian doctrines.

Large numbers of foreign missionaries had been working in China since the beginning of the nineteenth century, so Christianity had to be handled carefully. Chinese Christians were considered if not actual, then potential, foreign agents, as well as ideological subversives. It is undeniably true that the aggression of Western powers toward China—from 1839, when the Opium War that forced China to open trading ports to the West began, until World War II, when the main enemy in Asia for China, as well as for the West, was Japan—had benefited Western Christian missionaries in their attempts to win Chinese converts. The Communists, therefore, might be forgiven for viewing and resenting missionaries as "ideological allies" of Western imperialists. In reality, though, many Western missionaries not only opposed their nations' aggression towards China, they also served China with exceptional unselfishness and dedication. Nonetheless, within a few years after the Communists took power, all the foreign missionaries were expelled, and the Chinese Christians who remained were on their own and at the mercy of a state whose official ideology, being Marxist-Leninist, was totally opposed to religion. When

Mao Tse-tung succumbed to the temptation of all dictatorial leaders of atheist regimes to be treated as a deity, especially during the nightmare of the 1966–1976 Cultural Revolution, these Christians were cruelly persecuted.[40]

Atheist dictators, it must be said, seem to have a paranoia about being number two on any devotee's adoration list. In the Soviet Union, North Korea, Eastern Europe, China, and probably in Vietnam too, atheist regimes have shown themselves threatened not just by any sign of political opposition—which they usually have no difficulty in suppressing—but by any sign of "spiritual" dissent. They are profoundly disquieted by the thought that ordinary people might have some spiritual source of alliance other than the "Great Leader," or the "Great Helmsman" (which was how Mao was known during the Cultural Revolution), or The Party, or whatever human entity where ultimate moral authority is supposed to reside in the pinched-in universe of atheism. Thus, when Chinese Christian leader Li Tian'en was arrested in 1960 for allegedly committing a "counter-revolutionary" crime and shipped off to an iron-ore mine in coastal Anhui Province, the camp authorities were not content with simply subjecting him to a fierce regime of daily forced labor. It was essential to force him, if possible, to surrender his entirely private spiritual allegiances as well. To that end, they assigned two prisoners to cell beds next to him to watch his lips at night, to ensure that he didn't pray. Of course, he did, and was punished by being forced to stand against a wall, sometimes in winter, without a shirt, for up to six hours.[41]

Unlike Kim Il Sung, Mao Tse-tung had no known exposure as a child or youth to Christian teaching. As a young man, however, he studied extensively the foreign translations of recent contemporary Western philosophers while working as an assistant librarian at Peking University, the nation's best. One of the books he read, and annotated extensively, was *A System of Ethics* by the late-nineteenth-century German philosopher Friedrich Paulsen. An educator and a philosopher, Paulsen was an atheist who held that the soul was an objective reality that could be known through the act of will, where will is understood as an often-subconscious instinct rather than the more common view of "rational desire." In the margins of Paulsen's work, Mao wrote, "I do not agree with the view that to be moral, the motive of one's action has to be benefiting others. Morality does not have to be defined in relation to others. . . . People like me want to . . . satisfy our hearts to the full, and in doing so we automatically have the most valuable moral codes. Of course, there are people and objects in the world, but they are all there only for me." He also wrote, "People like me only have a duty to ourselves; we have no duty to other people. . . . I am responsible only for the reality that I know, and absolutely not responsible for anything else."[42]

It is hard to imagine a more unadulterated display of moral selfishness on the part of any recent world leader. Such a philosophy is clearly antipathetic to traditional Confucianism, which emphasizes reciprocal obligations and duties at all levels of society. It is in fact transparently atheistic. Where did

Mao acquire this outlook? Well, any person can, of course, be entirely self-centered and egotistical regardless of his beliefs. But Mao's personal philosophy was at the very least unmistakably reinforced by, if not directly learned from, a German atheist philosopher who had in turn acquired *his* philosophy from predecessors like Feuerbach and Marx.

The last—and mercifully, for the Cambodian people, the most short-lived—of the atheist dictators to come to power in the twentieth century was Pol Pot (1925–1998), who ruled the revolutionary state of Democratic Kampuchea from 1975 until 1979, when he was overthrown by the invading Vietnamese. Even after he was out of power, though, Pol Pot hovered like a terrifying specter of evil over Cambodian national affairs and was only finally arrested in 1997 by some dissident underlings. He died the following year before the international community could put him on trial for genocide.

Pol Pot was probably the most extreme practitioner of the ultimate in Marxist social experimentation to take power. After the Khmer Rouge Communists took over Cambodia in April 1975, they emptied every single city in the nation at gunpoint and relocated the residents to collective farms in the countryside to perform slave labor. These captives endured an almost unimaginably brutal existence, put on starvation rations of two bowls of rice soup a day, and subjected to random executions for crimes ranging from "stealing" food from the fields to wearing reading glasses and thus being an "intellectual." Cannibalism was common as people became more and more desperate for food. In some cases, the regime murdered people so that their bodies could be used for fertilizer. In many, perhaps most, cases of execution, the victims were not shot but beaten to death with farming tools. In other cases, to save the cost of a bullet, victims were suffocated to death with a plastic bag tied over their heads.

Pol Pot had acquired his Marxism (and atheism) as a student in Paris from French teachers and philosophers such as Jean-Paul Sartre and Maurice Merleau-Ponty who, at the time, were often slavish apologists for Stalin and indeed defenders of terror in the name of "humanism."[43] But Pol Pot displayed a level of demonic malevolence in the hell he imposed upon his country that begs the question of whether mere disbelief in a deity is sufficient to account for the evil that is committed once all moral restraint filtering down from a society's religious and moral traditions has been repudiated. (In Cambodia's case, the religious tradition was Buddhism.) Pol Pot wished to be the ultimate revolutionary, higher in the pantheon of world revolutionaries than even Marx, Lenin, or Mao. "The Khmer revolution has no predecessors. What we are trying to bring about has never been accomplished at any time in history," was the way the Khmers Rouges sometimes explained their extremist approach.[44] And indeed, they did try to outdo what earlier revolutionaries had done.

Because Marx had criticized the use of money, the central bank in Phnom Penh was literally blown up. The calendar was changed, just as it had been in France during the French

Revolution, so that 1975 was "The Year Zero." "We are making a unique revolution, is there any other country that would dare abolish money and markets the way we have?" said a Cambodian revolutionary.[45] In fact, of all the revolutionary experiments previously tried, Cambodia's was closest to that of Maoist China. It is interesting, therefore, that the assessment of Pol Pot's character offered by his brother-in-law, the powerful Khmer Rouge leader Ieng Sary, was this: "Pol Pot thought that he was above everyone else on the whole planet. He was a god on earth."[46]

The number of deaths Pol Pot was responsible for in the years the Khmer Communists ruled Cambodia may never be known. Estimates have ranged from 1.2 million to 2 million, of a total population in 1975 of 7.3 million. The Communist regimes of the Soviet Union, China, North Korea, Vietnam, Africa, Afghanistan, and those in Eastern Europe and Latin America have, between them, disposed of about 90 million more people. Some observers have concluded that one of the reasons for the murderous ferocity of communist regimes was the "scientism" of their rulers, the same scientism that we just encountered in the previous chapter. The Franco-Bulgarian philosopher Tzvetan Todorov, a thoughtful commentator on totalitarian terror, observed: "It was scientism and not humanism that helped establish the ideological bases of totalitarianism. . . . One must already be a practitioner of scientism, even if it is 'wild' scientism, to believe in the perfect transparency of society and thus in the possibility of transforming society by revolutionary means to conform with an ideal."[47] Of course, the "scientism" of the Marxist-Leninists was a deluded belief that a nineteenth-century bearded German philosopher living in London had discovered the laws of history in the same way that the law of universal gravitation had been discovered by Sir Isaac Newton. As *The Black Book of Communism: Crimes, Terror and Repression* observed, "Marx had a redemptive belief in the Promethean destiny of mankind." That is, he had a messianic vision that the world, as the eminent Polish philosopher Leszek Kolakowski put it, "is so totally corrupt that it is beyond improvement" and therefore must be destroyed.[48]

Ernest Renan (1823–1892), a noted French philosopher—and critic of the Bible—speculated that the way to achieve absolute power in an atheist society was not to threaten people with a mythological hell, but to institute a real one, a giant concentration camp to intimidate opponents, and moreover, one policed by robotic enforcers of regime tyranny.[49] Other commentators on atheist totalitarianism have noted that regimes often succeed in exterminating opponents not simply by dehumanizing them but by describing them as animals—or even more sinisterly as vermin or insects against which society needs to be disinfected. That kind of thinking brings us back to the idea of religion as a "virus," the great "discovery" of Dawkins and his disciple, Dennett.

Finally, because he ranted against the "vermin" of his day, we are also back to Hitler. It is impossible to discuss Hitler without reference to the German philosopher who influenced him uniquely, namely Friedrich Nietzsche (1844–1900). Hitler kept a bust of Nietzsche in his office, and he even gave a copy of one of Nietzsche's works to the Italian dictator Benito Mussolini (who reportedly did not read it). Nietzsche's philosophy has been interpreted in several ways since his death. He referred to himself as the Antichrist, but he is probably most famous for the passage from his book *The Joyful Wisdom* (the title was originally translated as *The Gay Science*, but it needs to be stressed that at the time of the work's writing, in the 1880s, the word *gay* had no connotation in general usage of "homosexual"). In the book, Nietzsche first tells the parable of a madman who runs into a town marketplace and declares, "God is dead! God remains dead! And we have killed him!" Nietzsche then explains the meaning of this odd tale: "The most important of more recent events—that 'God is dead,' that the belief in the Christian God has become unworthy of belief—already begins to cast its first shadows over Europe."[50] In fact, Nietzsche went on to predict that the twentieth century would be the bloodiest ever, precisely because of the waning of cultural and moral restraints resulting from Christianity's diminishing influence.

Nietzsche himself admired the personality of Jesus but considered Christianity a religion for weaklings. In other words, he advanced the idea of a human superman—in German, *Übermensch*—who would be beyond considerations of right or wrong in all his actions. Hitler was profoundly influenced by the ideas of Nietzsche, though his antagonism for the Jews came not from Nietzsche but primarily from the writings of the composer Richard Wagner (1813–1883). In Hitler's auto-biography *Mein Kampf*, published in 1925, this antagonism toward the Jews is quite evident, along with a contempt for both Protestant and Roman Catholic Christians in Germany for opposing the Nazi policy of planning to sterilize "syphilitics . . . cripples, and imbeciles."

A much more revealing glimpse of Hitler's innermost atti-tudes, however, is found in *Table Talk*, the transcript of con-versations Hitler held with his senior aides intermittently from 1941 to 1944. Hitler's comments were taken down in German shorthand by a German officer who knew stenography. In *Table Talk*, Hitler made it quite plain that he had nothing but con-tempt for the core beliefs of Christianity. "The heaviest blow that ever struck humanity was the coming of Christianity," he said in one conversation. "Bolshevism is Christianity's ille-gitimate child. Both are inventions of the Jew. The deliberate lie in the matter of religion was introduced into the world by Christianity. . . . Taken to its logical extreme, Christianity would mean the systematic cultivation of the human failure." And there is this:

> The reason why the ancient world was so pure, light, and serene was that it knew nothing of the two great scourges: the pox and Christianity. . . . The Jew who fraudulently introduced Christianity into the ancient world—in order to ruin it—re-opened the same breach in modern times,

taking as his pretext the social question. Just as Saul became St. Paul, Mardochai has become Karl Marx. . . . Christianity is an invention of sick brains. . . . The war will be over one day. I shall then consider my life's final task will be to solve the religious problem.[51]

Hitler made sure that the special contempt he nurtured for Christianity as a religion for weaklings was not exclusive to him alone. In Hitler Youth summer camps in the 1930s, the teenagers were encouraged to sing the Horst Wessel song, a paean to a Nazi who had been murdered by German Communists during a demonstration. But they also sang a song that was specifically designed to contrast the hopes for Germany supposedly nourished by Nazism with the Christian faith. One chorus went:

We follow not Christ, but Horst Wessel,
Away with incense and Holy Water,
The Church can go hang for all we care,
The Swastika brings salvation on Earth.[52]

The revelations of Hitler's most closely held views do not contradict the fact that he never renounced his Catholicism and never declared himself to be either an atheist or an agnostic. He didn't need to; the inhumane policy toward society's weaker members in the 1930s spelled out exactly what *Mein Kampf* had revealed in the 1920s would be his policy. Hitler was in practice a man who acted as though there were no external moral constraints on any of his actions; he acted out his policies as though atheism were true. His was a clear case of actions speaking louder than words.

Sam Harris, in *Letter to a Christian Nation*, makes the claim that knowledge of the "psychological laws that govern human well-being" will eventually provide "an enduring basis for an objective morality." He adds the banal notation that "raping and killing our neighbors is not one of its primary constituents" and that love is "more conducive to happiness than hate is." Well, you don't have to be a Stanford graduate to figure that out. But then Harris makes a gigantic leap in moral reasoning. "It is clearly possible to say," he asserts, "that someone like Hitler was wrong in moral terms without reference to scripture."[53] Well, let's leave out Scripture for the time being. There are surely very few people in the world who would in polite company proclaim Hitler to be anything but incalculably wicked. The awkward fact, however, is that it is exceptionally difficult to define "wicked" in a precise way without reference to some transcendent moral authority of good or evil. No sane person wants to defend what Hitler did. But Hitler didn't just happen; he was the product of a shifting moral environment in European culture, a shift that was based on the emphatic rejection of the absolutes of Christianity (and indeed of Judaism as well).

That shift took place during a dramatic philosophical reorientation in Europe birthed in the mid-eighteenth-century

Enlightenment and culminating some 150 years later in Nietzsche's extreme denunciations of belief in God. It is a signal mark of how the United States has been historically blessed (whether or not you want to believe that there is a God who does the blessing) that it escaped this shift. Nietzsche's ethical nihilism and Lenin's depraved revolutionary utilitarianism gained hardly any traction at all in American culture. With all due respect to Hitchens's and Thomas Jefferson's hostility to conventional beliefs about the deity, the reason the United States remained largely untouched by Nietzsche's and Lenin's philosophies is because its founding was rooted in an emphatically Christian worldview.

# Chapter Six

# THE
# CHRISTIAN WORLDVIEW
## IS THE
# FOUNDATION OF LIBERTY

*"Can an atheist be a good citizen? That has been done,
many times. Can American liberties survive if most of
our nation is atheist? The most common, almost universal
judgment of the founders was that it could not."*
— Michael Novak, 1998[1]

The Four Horsemen make some rash statements in their
books, and they are guilty of distortions, unbalanced
generalizations, and downright factual errors. But the utter
ignorance of American history displayed by Oxford professor
Richard Dawkins is nothing short of astonishing. Christopher
Hitchens is more measured on the subject of the Founding
Fathers, probably because he's written two impressive short
monographs: one on Thomas Jefferson, who was one of
America's greatest presidents, and the other on the nation's
most famous and controversial (and probably most influential) pamphleteer, Thomas Paine. Dawkins, on the other hand,

displays breathtaking self-assurance in an area for which he is not known to have the slightest expertise, and he makes some observations about American history that are so ludicrous they have surely embarrassed his Oxford colleagues in the field of history.

Such ignorance might not matter that much except for one very important point, which was examined in the previous chapter: Atheism, when adopted wholesale by any government or society, has very profound and—as was evident in the twentieth century—disturbing consequences for political liberty. Every single one of the Founding Fathers understood this, which makes Dawkins's judgments of Revolutionary-era America and its leaders almost incomprehensible in light of the real historical evidence. "It has been argued that the greatest of them might have been atheists," he writes of the Founders. "Certainly their writings on religion in their own time leave me in no doubt that most of them would have been atheists in ours. But whatever their individual religious views in their own time, the one thing they collectively were is *secularists*. . . ."[2] Hitchens, obviously much better-read than Dawkins about early America, refrains from this folly, contenting himself only with the suggestion that Jefferson and Benjamin Franklin "managed to seize a moment of crisis and use it to enshrine Enlightenment values in the founding documents of the United States of America."[3] The exact meaning of "Enlightenment values" will be considered shortly.

The strongest argument Hitchens makes that the Founders

were not men of faith is that, almost to a man, none had a priest at his deathbed. In this, Hitchens displays *his* ignorance: Dying Protestants don't make a habit of calling on priests to attend their departure from this life. Hitchens is probably thinking of Roman Catholic "last rites," a practice among faithful Catholics who want a priest to absolve them of their sins before they die. (In fact, Founding Father and Protestant Alexander Hamilton *did* receive absolution for his sin of dueling from the Episcopal Bishop of New York as he lay dying from the fatal gunshot wound dealt him by his longtime political rival Aaron Burr on July 11, 1804. But Hamilton was indeed a rarity.)

As every American schoolchild knows, before the Founding Fathers, there were the Pilgrims, with whom Thanksgiving is indelibly associated. Standard history textbooks agree that the first Thanksgiving was a celebration of thanks to God for his care of and provision for the band of intrepid settlers through their difficult first year. The history books also agree on the fact that the impetus for the Pilgrims' 1620 journey from England to a dangerous unknown world was their desire for religious freedom. After anchoring off what is today Massachusetts, they drafted and signed the Mayflower Compact, which was both a religious and a civil covenant to guide the second permanent English settlement in North America (the first of which was in Jamestown, Virginia). The document explains itself in these terms:

> We whose names are under-written, . . . Having undertaken, for the Glory of God and advancement of the Christian

Faith and Honour of our King and Country, a Voyage to plant the First Colony in the Northern Parts of Virginia, do by these presents solemnly and mutually in the presence of God and one of another, Covenant and Combine ourselves together into a Civil Body Politic, for our better ordering and preservation and furtherance of the ends aforesaid; and by virtue hereof to enact, constitute and frame such just and equal Laws, Ordinances, Acts, Constitutions and Offices, from time to time, as shall be thought most meet and convenient for the general good of the Colony, unto which we promise all due submission and obedience.[4]

Starting with this first document in American history, often referred to as the foundation of the U.S. Constitution, the Christian purpose of the United States has been woven through the warp and woof of every major constitutional document that has followed—a fact that has been taught to American schoolchildren through the ages but which apparently escaped the notice of Oxford professor Dawkins.

Dawkins's ignorance about American history is even more evident when he comments on the fact that Great Britain, which has a state church, is notably more secular than the United States, whose Constitution bans government establishment of any religion. "I am continually asked why this is," he says with evident perplexity, "and I do not know."[5] Any American college student with exposure to the writing of Frenchmen Alexis de Tocqueville could answer that question easily, as we shall see.

Dawkins contents himself with the odd notion that the British are less religious these days because "England has wearied of religion after an appalling history of inter-faith violence, with Protestants and Catholics alternately gaining the upper hand and systematically murdering the other lot."[6] This only reveals Dawkins's failure to comprehend English history.

One of England's greatest Christian revival movements was the Wesleyan Revival, also known as the Methodist Revival, which dramatically altered social habits beginning in the last quarter of the eighteenth century. Moreover, it resulted in some momentous developments in British history. For example, the man who led the campaign and indeed devoted his life to ending the British slave trade, William Wilberforce (1759–1833), was converted in 1785 to evangelical Christianity during that revival.[7] That same revival produced Victorian evangelical Christianity, which made Great Britain for a time the most zealously Christian society in Europe. Clearly, if the English of the mid-eighteenth century had been as similarly "wearied" by the Protestant-Catholic conflicts as Dawkins believes today's Britons are, these dramatic changes could never have occurred.

It was during this same historical period, which has since come to be known as "the Enlightenment," that America was embroiled in fighting its War of Independence and its Founding Fathers were grappling with the debate over the fledgling nation's Constitution. The intellectual thinking of the Enlightenment years was characterized by an emphasis on reason and science, and this was particularly evident in Europe in a sustained assault upon revealed religion, especially Christianity with its traditional beliefs about the Bible and about Jesus Christ. Most of the American founders, and particularly Thomas Jefferson, were deeply steeped in Enlightenment thinking about the rights of man, the notion of a social contract in the governance of society, and indeed an atmosphere of general skepticism toward the Christian church as an institution. One of the religious beliefs that became popular among intellectuals on both sides of the Atlantic was deism, the view that a divine Creator does exist but his function was simply to set the universe in motion and then to step back from it.

Some of America's forefathers had grave doubts about both traditional Christianity's claims to the truth and the historical role of the church and its officers. Jefferson, Franklin, Hamilton, James Madison, and John Adams often made biting comments about Christian clergy and Christian doctrines—especially those making supernatural claims—and about the role of the church in society. In spite of this, it is clear from their actions in life and from their writings that the founders were overwhelmingly *not* deists, let alone atheists. "Secular" they certainly were, but only in the sense that they did not want ecclesiastical institutions to play any role in politics and government. As the American Catholic philosopher and diplomat Michael Novak elegantly points out in his excellent book *On Two Wings: Humble Faith and Common Sense at the American Founding*, while all of the Founding Fathers held reason in very high regard in the establishment of a new, independent republic in America, it is striking how much they still embraced Protestant Christianity's basic worldview, a way of thinking that had its roots in both the Puritans and the First Great Awakening, which swept across America in the 1730s and 1740s. "Virtually all the signers of the Declaration and Constitution were churchgoing men," Novak points out. Furthermore, several were ordained, some had trained to be ministers, and a few were conspicuously well-versed in religious matters. Of the fifty-six signers of the Declaration, thirty-four were Anglicans, thirteen Congregationalists (originally known as Puritans), six Presbyterian, one Catholic, one Baptist, and one Quaker. According to Novak, "nearly the same" proportions applied to the thirty-nine men who signed the Constitution.[8]

By contrast, the English-born Thomas Paine (1737–1809) stands out as the most outspoken of all the revolutionary-era anti-Christians in America. The brilliant propagandist for independence in his work *Common Sense* (1776), and then the much more controversial adversary of Christianity and the Bible in *The Age of Reason* (1793–1794), Paine was nevertheless emphatically *not* an atheist. In fact, one of the reasons he sailed for France after the French Revolution began in 1789 was to *fight against* atheism, which he rightly held was later significantly responsible for the massacres of the French Revolution's 1793–1794 Reign of Terror. Paine never failed to emphasize that he did not hold to any traditional Christian beliefs; for that matter, he rejected the creeds "expressed by the Jewish Church, by the Roman Church, by the Greek Church, by the Turkish Church, by the Protestant Church, [and] by any church that I know of. My mind is my own church."[9] In France, Paine gravitated towards Freemasonry and "theophilanthropy," an eclectic set of beliefs based on deism that was briefly popular among intellectuals in Paris who sought to install it as a state religion instead of Catholicism.

In *The Age of Reason*, Paine wrote that he aspired to happiness "beyond this life" and believed in religious duties that consisted of "doing justice, loving mercy, and endeavoring to make our fellow-creatures happy." That formulation sounds pretty biblical, in fact, and is nearly identical to what the Bible says in Micah 6:8: "He has showed you, O man, what is good. And what does the LORD require of you? To act justly and to love mercy and to walk humbly with your God." By 1797, Paine had redirected his rhetorical guns away from the Bible and Christianity and aimed them at atheism instead. "Religion has two principal enemies," he wrote, "fanaticism and infidelity, or that which is called atheism. . . . The existence of a God is the first dogma of the Theophilanthropists."[10]

Of all the Founding Fathers and leaders of America's great experiment with liberty, Thomas Jefferson was unquestionably the most hostile toward Christianity. Rather than being a deist, let alone an atheist, however, he was closer to being a Unitarian, which in those days meant someone who believed in God but not the Trinity. The term carried none of today's connotation of someone who doesn't really believe in God at all. Dawkins cites with great approval from fellow atheist Hitchens's book on Jefferson[11] the president's letter to his nephew, Peter Carr, in which he advises, "Shake off all the fears of servile prejudices under which weak minds are servilely crouched. Fix reason firmly in her seat, and call to her tribunal every fact, every opinion. Question with boldness even the existence of a God; because, if there be one, he must more approve of the homage of reason than that of blindfolded fear."[12] Dawkins implies that, by encouraging Carr to question everything, Jefferson himself had come to the conclusion God doesn't exist.

Nothing could be further from the truth. It is true that Jefferson was hostile to biblical Christianity and its assertions of the miraculous; he certainly didn't believe Jesus was either divine or had been raised from the dead. For his own amusement, Jefferson had literally cut out of the Gospels anything that smacked of the supernatural. He admired the *philosophes*, the eighteenth-century Enlightenment intellectuals in France. He was in Paris when the Bastille fell to the French insurrectionists on July 14, 1789, and was noticeably more sympathetic to the French Revolution, even after it entered its most bloodthirsty phase, than any other of his American fellow revolutionaries. But while Jefferson was hostile to Christianity both in the forms it took in the America of his day and in its historical expressions, he was happy to call himself a Christian in the sense of one who aspired to the values of Jesus Christ. "To the corruptions of Christianity I am indeed opposed; but not to the genuine precepts of Jesus himself," he wrote in a letter to Benjamin Rush (1745–1813), a fellow signer of the Declaration and a man of devout Christian faith. "I am a Christian, in the only sense he wished any one to be; sincerely attached to his doctrines, in preference to all others; ascribing to himself every human excellence; and believing he never claimed other."[13]

Jefferson believed in God's intervention in human affairs, a viewpoint that was very far from deism. Although a slave owner, he was opposed to slavery and famously said of slavery, "Can the liberties of a nation be thought secure when we have removed their only firm basis, a conviction in the minds of the people that these liberties are the gift of God? That they are not to be violated but with his wrath? Indeed, I tremble for my country when I reflect that God is just: that His justice cannot sleep forever. . . ."[14] The God whose justice doesn't sleep is an interventionist God, not a deist one.

Jefferson, while rejecting the core doctrines of Christianity, nevertheless was convinced that adherence to them was not just useful but essential for democratic life to succeed in the newly independent America. During his 1801–1809 presidency, he arranged for Christian worship services to be held in the Capitol itself—a breach of church-state separation if ever there was one—and took care to be a prominent participant at those services. This led to an incident narrated by the Rev. Ethan Allen (1797–1879) in which a minister encountered Jefferson on the way to church, red prayer book under arm, and asked where he was going.

"Church Sir," Jefferson replied.

"You going to church?" the minister retorted. "You do not believe a word in it."

"Sir," Jefferson replied, "no nation has ever yet existed or been governed without religion. Nor can be. The Christian religion is the best religion that has ever been given to man and I as chief Magistrate of this nation am bound to give it the sanction of my example. Good morning Sir."[15]

Although there is some dispute over the veracity of Allen's account, the fact that Jefferson publicly supported the Christian religion, that as president he signed bills appropriating federal funding for chaplains and missionaries, and that, laboring fondly in retirement over his plans for the University of Virginia, he set aside a site in the Rotunda partly as a place to hold religious services all indicate that, whatever his private reservations about Christianity's doctrinal veracity, he was convinced that Christian worship in diverse denominational ways should be encouraged.

Benjamin Franklin, the prodigious inventor and diplomat, is often held up as another of the most respected Founding Fathers who didn't identify himself as a Christian. Yet it was Franklin who, on June 28, 1787, appealed to the delegates of the Constitutional Convention in Philadelphia that they collectively turn to prayer after more than a month of such bitter discussions that some of the fifty-five Convention delegates had started to leave. Eighty-one-year-old Franklin said, "I have lived, Sir, a long time and the longer I live, the more convincing proofs I see of this truth—that <u>God</u> *governs in the affairs of men*. And if a sparrow cannot fall to the ground without His notice, is it probable that an empire can rise without His aid?" (emphasis in the original).[16]

Many of the Founding Fathers shared this strong belief in the need to give public support to Christianity in general; in essence, they believed that whether Christianity were true or not, by encouraging virtue, it served a vital service to society in protecting the new republic. Later in Jefferson's life, during a long and amicable correspondence with his presidential predecessor, John Adams, the two men compared notes on the value—or lack of it—that religion contributed to society. "Twenty times, during my late reading, have I been upon the point of breaking out, 'This would be the best of all possible Worlds, if there was no Religion in it'!!! But in this exclamatic I should have been as fanatical as Bryant or Cleverly," Adams wrote. He was referring to the endless arguments over religious and political matters that his former Latin schoolmaster, Joseph Cleverly, whom he describes as "a bigoted episcopalian," carried on with his former parish priest and "liberal Scholar," Lemuel Bryant. "Without Religion, this World would be Something not fit to be mentioned in polite Company, I mean Hell."[17] Jefferson replied, less than three weeks later, "If, by *religion*, we are to understand *Sectarian dogmas*, in which no two of them agree, then your exclamation on that hypothesis is just, 'that this would be the best of all possible worlds, if there were no religion in it.' But if the moral precepts, innate in man, and made a part of his physical constitution, as necessary for a social being, if the sublime doctrines of philanthropism, and deism taught us by Jesus of Nazareth in which all agree, constitute true religion, then, without it, this would be, as you again say, 'something not fit to be named, even indeed a Hell.'"[18]

With the hindsight of two centuries, the anxieties of the framers of the Constitution over how to avoid such a "hell" might seem ill-placed given America's phenomenal success over the past 220 years as an orderly, constitutional nation—the blight of slavery and the Civil War being obvious unpleasant exceptions. To the fifty-five delegates who convened in Philadelphia that hot summer of 1787, however, the signal failure of previous experiments in republican government to survive for more than a few decades at a time was very real. Those earlier experiments in nonautocratic government ultimately collapsed because of the character flaws of the citizenry charged with making them work. The Constitutional Convention delegates all were well aware that character formation was essential to the process of both creating liberty and ordering liberty and that legal processes alone were not enough. Describing how a consensus emerged on a republican-style government, several commentators have stressed the relationship that the Founders seemed to envisage of freedom, virtue, and religion:

> Freedom needs virtue in order to be sustained;
> Virtue needs the reinforcement of religion;

Religion, to be effective in influencing people, has to be free.[19]

The physician and writer Benjamin Rush, a signatory to the Declaration of Independence and a member of the Continental Congress, expressed this principle in 1798, writing, "[T]he only foundation for a useful education in a republic is to be laid in Religion. Without this there can be no virtue, and without virtue there can be no liberty, and liberty is the object and life of all republican governments."[20] He added, "Such is my veneration for every religion that reveals the attributes of the Deity, or a future state of rewards and punishments, that I had rather see the opinions of Confucius or Mahomed inculcated upon our youth, than see them grow up wholly devoid of a system of religious principles. But the religion I mean to recommend," he insisted, "is that of the New Testament."[21] Rush made it clear that his purpose was not to evangelize on behalf of Christianity. "It is foreign to my purposes to hint at the arguments which establish the truth of the Christian revelation," he explained. "My only business is to declare, that all its doctrines and precepts are calculated to promote the happiness of society, and the safety and well being of civil government."[22]

Without question, the most influential clergyman among the Founders was John Witherspoon, the president of Princeton University, originally called the College of New Jersey. Witherspoon's views greatly influenced the young nation's first leaders, and Adams described him as "as high a son of liberty as any man in America."[23] Witherspoon had for years sat on the fence theologically on the issue of independence from Britain, but had finally come down decisively in favor of it in a May 17, 1776, sermon preached at the College of New Jersey. In that sermon, which has since been reprinted repeatedly, Witherspoon warned of the danger facing the new republic if virtue were lacking: "Nothing is more certain than that a general profligacy and corruption of manners make a people ripe for destruction. A good form of government may hold the rotten materials together for some time, but beyond a certain pitch, even the best constitution will be ineffectual, and slavery must ensue."[24] Liberty, Witherspoon put it again and again, was God's gift to mankind. It had to be nurtured by human virtue.

Witherspoon's influence on his fellow signatories of the Declaration of Independence and on the subsequent signatories of the Constitution was quite simply incalculable. A professor of history, divinity, and eloquence, his moral philosophy class was a required course at the College of New Jersey. His former students included one U.S. president, one vice president, two foreign ministers, three attorneys general, three Supreme Court justices, five delegates to the Constitutional Convention, ten cabinet officers, twelve members of the Continental Congress, twenty-eight U.S. senators, forty-nine U.S. representatives, and dozens of military and civilian officials in the young American republic.

One of Witherspoon's most distinguished students went on

to be the fourth president of the United States. James Madison (1751–1836) had stayed on an extra year after his 1774 graduation in order to study under the Scottish-born Witherspoon. Madison believed as firmly as Witherspoon did in freedom of conscience, and the right of magistrates to defend it. It was Madison who penned the first draft of the Bill of Rights, and he vigorously and strategically pushed for its passage in the First U.S. Congress when it convened in 1789. It is noteworthy that of these first ten amendments to the Constitution, Madison made the First Amendment the bedrock of both religious liberty and freedom of the press in the United States. Madison was convinced that freedom was dependent on the virtue of the citizenry. As he told the Virginia Ratifying Convention that met in 1788 to consider the state constitution, "To suppose that any form of government will secure liberty or happiness without any virtue in the people, is a chimerical idea. If there be sufficient virtue and intelligence in the community, it will be exercised in the selection of these men; so that we do not depend on their virtue, or put confidence in our rulers, but in the people who are to choose them."[25]

Madison was not alone in his conviction of the unalterable link between freedom and virtue. Franklin observed, "Only a virtuous people are capable of freedom."[26] That sentiment, with only slightly different wording, could have come from virtually any of the other Founding Fathers. John Adams, America's second president, said in a 1789 address to the military, "Our Constitution was made only for a moral and religious people."[27] In a letter to a clergyman cousin, Adams expanded on this thought thus:

> Statesmen, my dear Sir, may plan and speculate for Liberty, but it is Religion and Morality alone, which can establish the Principles upon which Freedom can securely stand. The only foundation of a free Constitution, is pure Virtue, and if this cannot be inspired into our People in a great Measure, that they have it now, they may change their Rulers, and the forms of Government, but they will not obtain a lasting Liberty.[28]

In this view, Adams's thinking stood in stark contrast with that of one of the most prominent atheists of the French Enlightenment: the Marquis de Condorcet (1743–1794), a good friend of both Jefferson and Franklin. Condorcet argued that the foundation of morality was the "natural equality of mankind"—essentially the same view held by both Sam Harris and Christopher Hitchens. Harris argues: "Everything about human experience suggests that love is more conducive to happiness than hate is. This is an *objective* claim about the human mind, about the dynamics of social relations, and about the moral order of our world."[29] Harris's utopian belief in humankind's inherent goodness is directly contradicted by the life of a fellow atheist, the late Madalyn Murray O'Hair, who, as we shall see in the concluding chapter, thought it perfectly acceptable to make hateful statements about individuals or groups whom she detested. Hitchens doesn't make any generalizations like Harris's on the subject of love and hate, but he is quite dogmatic about his belief in the commonality of human ethics. In his concluding chapter, Hitchens appeals for a "renewed Enlightenment"—whatever that is supposed to mean—that he says will not depend on "the heroic breakthroughs of a few gifted and exceptionally courageous people." Rather, Hitchens proposes, this new Enlightenment "is within the compass of the average person."[30]

John Adams had no such illusions. Though definitely a man of the Enlightenment, he strongly disagreed with Condorcet, and indeed, implicitly with Hitchens's assertion in a *Washington Post* op-ed piece that "human solidarity [is] in some way innate."[31] Adams wrote in the margin of Condorcet's text, "There is no such thing [as morality] without the supposition of God. There is no right and wrong in the universe without the supposition of a moral government and an intellectual and moral governor."[32] Condorcet—as antireligious in the eighteenth century as Christopher Hitchens is in the twenty-first—argued that "religious superstition" had suppressed human genius. Adams responded, "But was there no genius among the Hebrews? None among the Christians, nor Mahometans? I understand you, Condorcet. It is atheistic genius alone that you would honor or tolerate."[33]

Although many of America's forefathers were dubious about Christianity's various doctrinal and indeed exclusive claims to truth, they embraced generic, nonsectarian Protestantism insofar as it seemed to encapsulate their concepts of Providence, divine justice, and morality. More than any other Founding Father, George Washington embodied the ideal of a wise, non-partisan follower of divine truth. He took painstaking care not to identify himself too closely with any Protestant denomination. Though he regularly attended Anglican Sunday church services, he seldom received Communion. He cultivated excellent relations with America's tiny Jewish community and the Roman Catholics. He was reticent about his own personal religious beliefs to the point almost of Delphic vagueness. When he died, no clergy was at his bedside, nor did he utter any expression of Christian orthodoxy.

But by his actions and in the orders he gave as commander in chief of the Continental Army, Washington made it abundantly clear that he believed in Providence, that is, in a deity who was actively involved in the affairs of nations. He believed that the elected leaders of the American people owed Providence recognition for blessing their nation and for rewarding virtue and punishing vice. Washington thus requested that chaplains be appointed within the Continental Army and that they organize religious services. He voiced his distress over the spread of profane speech among the men, and said he hoped that the officers would "by example, as well as influence, endeavor to check it." Washington was personally offended by profanity, which he called "a vice so mean and low . . . that every man of sense, and character, detests and despises it."[34]

In 1789, six years after the victory of the Revolutionary

War, and with the Constitution newly ratified and the constitutional government just beginning operations, Washington issued America's first national Thanksgiving Proclamation. It summed up the thinking of many—perhaps most—Americans of the day: The events that had resulted first in independence from Great Britain and then in the formation of a republican government were none other than the working of Providence in America's national life.

> Whereas it is the duty of all Nations to acknowledge the providence of Almighty God, to obey his will, to be grateful for his benefits, and humbly to implore his protection and favor . . . now therefore do I recommend and assign Thursday the 26th day of November next to be devoted by the People of these States to the service of that great and glorious Being, who is the beneficent Author of all the good that was, that is, or that will be. . . .[35]

There is nothing manipulative about this statement, and indeed nothing that would qualify as preachy or sectarian. That America had been miraculously delivered from foreign conquest and then set on a course of grand experiment in republican living was plain to everyone.

From these and other generic references to Providence, the Supreme Being, or a Grand Architect, one could classify Washington as either a deist or a Unitarian. But when he was recommending spiritual allegiance to the Indian chiefs of the

Delaware tribe, Washington was more outspokenly Christian, suggesting that they would do well to study and adopt "the religion of Jesus Christ." As president, he also sought government funding for Christian missionary efforts among Native Americans. But that was the furthest Washington was known to have gone in publicly identifying America's worldview as specifically Christian. By instinct, he seemed to prefer philosophical phraseology calculated not to cause offense either to particular Protestant or Catholic groups or, indeed, to the nascent American Jewish community, with whom he took care to cultivate good relations.

One of the most studied of Washington's writings was his Farewell Address, penned at the end of his second term as president. Both Alexander Hamilton and James Madison collaborated on this valedictory, but historians agree that the contents reflected Washington's thoughts, ideas, and principles. One of the key passages on religion and morality is worth quoting at some length. He wrote:

> Of all the dispositions and habits which lead to political prosperity, Religion and morality are indispensable supports. In vain would that man claim the tribute of Patriotism, who should labour to subvert these great Pillars of human happiness, these firmest props of the duties of Men and citizens. The mere Politician, equally with the pious man ought to respect & to cherish them. A volume could not trace all their connections with private and public felicity. . . . And let us

with caution indulge the supposition, that morality can be maintained without religion. Whatever may be conceded to the influence of refined education on minds of peculiar structure—reason & experience both forbid us to expect that National morality can prevail in exclusion of religious principle.

'Tis substantially true, that virtue or morality is a necessary spring of popular government. The rule indeed extends with more or less force to every species of Free Government. Who that is a sincere friend to it, can look with indifference upon attempts to shake the foundation of the fabric?[36]

Some historians believe the phrase "on minds of peculiar structure" was a deliberate dig at Thomas Jefferson for his doubts about the veracity of Christianity.

The founders were men of letters, both widely and well-read: in the writings of the Enlightenment, in the Greek and Latin classics, and in both Hebrew and the New Testament Scriptures. Which sources were most influential? It is hard to ignore the evidence that the Jewish and Christian Bible provided the clearest sources of inspiration to them. Scholars have looked at what the original source material was of the quotations in the Founders' writings, and they have discovered that by far the largest percentage came from the Bible: 34 percent. The next largest source, 22 percent, were the Enlightenment authors, and of them, the single most quoted author was the politically and socially moderate French commentator Charles Montesquieu, rather than any of the more radical Enlightenment thinkers.

Dawkins, in insisting that the early American republic had almost no Christian component, takes no notice of any of the ample historical evidence to the contrary, of which only a handful of noteworthy examples have been cited here. The only historical evidence that Dawkins points to that has any strength at all is the 1797 Treaty with Tripoli, an international agreement intended to placate the Muslim pirates who had been plying the Mediterranean for hundreds of years and regularly attacking Western merchant ships, including American. The treaty, which comes up all the time in debates about separation of church and state and about America as a Christian nation, was negotiated in 1796, and an English translation was prepared by the American consul Joel Barlow. Article 11 of the treaty contains the words that are the focus of so much debate even today:

> As the Government of the United States is not, in any sense, founded on the Christian religion; as it has in itself no character of enmity against the laws, religion, or tranquillity, or Mussulmen; and as the said States never entered into any war or act of hostility against any Mahometan nation, it is declared by the parties, that no pretext arising from religious opinions, shall ever produce an interruption of the harmony existing between the two countries.[37]

Several important points need to be made about Article 11. First, the Arabic version of the treaty does not include this article; it was part of the treaty's English translation only. This English version was what was read on the floor of the Senate, which unanimously adopted an advice-and-consent motion on it. Although the authorship of Article 11 is unclear, historians generally agree that it was most likely written by Barlow, who was known for being a deist and a strong advocate of separation of church and state. Second, the wording of Article 11 is technically correct in that the *government* of the United States has no established religion, and indeed is prohibited from having one by the First Amendment to the Constitution. Thus, when the Senate voted on the treaty, no dissenting vote was cast—because it accorded with the letter of the Constitution.

The final important point has to do with the historical background of the treaty. Muslim pirates had been preying on "Christian" merchant shipping in the Mediterranean for hundreds of years, in the process taking into slavery hundreds of thousands of people. The Muslim motivation was both financial and religious. It was financial because they reaped huge profits from the ransom that Western governments and individuals paid for the release of kidnapped compatriots. It was religious because Islamic *shariah* (religious law) encourages Islamic believers to wage war on non-Muslim peoples and, if possible, to enslave them. European states routinely paid huge annual fees to the Muslim pirates to prevent their merchant ships from being boarded and their men captured. For the just-established United States, which had no significant navy at the time and had lost British naval protection when it gained independence, claiming religious "neutrality" as part of an effort to forestall piracy was nothing more than a prudent and pragmatic strategy. When the United States was strong enough to respond militarily, President Jefferson called for war after the 1803 capture of three hundred American seamen. In 1804, U.S. ships bombarded Tripoli and set up a blockade. The following year, Tripoli sued for peace and, in the new treaty that was negotiated, Article 11 was entirely absent, although the document did say that the United States had no established church. The diplomatic convenience that was behind the Senate approval of the original treaty with its disavowal of America as a "Christian" nation was overtaken by events and was no longer necessary.

A far more powerful repudiation of Dawkins's assertion that the founding of the United States of America was not connected at its roots with Protestant Christianity, however, comes from the brilliant foreign observer who visited the still-young American republic in 1831. Alexis de Tocqueville (1805–1859) was a Frenchman and at least a nominal Roman Catholic whose original purpose for visiting the United States was to compare French and American penal systems. After returning to France in 1832, de Tocqueville wrote his masterwork, *Democracy in America*, in which he crystallized his thinking on why the young American republic and its citizens had so impressed him. He wrote:

On my arrival in America, the religious aspect of the country was the first thing that struck my attention; and the longer I stayed there, the more did I perceive the great political consequences resulting from this state of things. In France I had almost always seen the spirit of religion and the spirit of freedom pursuing courses diametrically opposed to each other; but in America I found they were intimately united, and that they reigned in common over the same country. . . .[38]

De Tocqueville astutely observed that freedom and religion were united in America for a common purpose—to maintain social order:

Hitherto no one in the United States has dared to advance the maxim, that everything is permissible for the interest of society; an impious adage which seems to have been invented in an age of freedom to shelter all the future tyrants of future ages. Thus whilst the law permits the Americans to do what they please, religion prevents them from conceiving, and forbids them to commit, what is rash or unjust. . . .[39]

The young Frenchman also quickly grasped that for the Americans he observed, Christian belief was no dry, dead set of creeds but an active force deep within them that was essential to the preservation of freedom.

The Americans combine the notions of Christianity and of liberty so intimately in their minds, that it is impossible to make them conceive the one without the other; and with them this conviction does not spring from that barren traditionary faith which seems to vegetate in the soul rather than to live.[40]

De Tocqueville came to the same conclusion that the Founding Fathers had: that without belief in God, an orderly moral society was doomed to fail. His closing words of this chapter entitled "Principal Causes Maintaining The Democratic Republic" were:

Despotism may govern without faith, but liberty cannot. Religion is much more necessary in the republic which they set forth in glowing colors than in the monarchy which they attack; and it is more needed in democratic republics than in any others. How is it possible that society should escape destruction if the moral tie be not strengthened in proportion as the political tie is relaxed? and what can be done with a people which is its own master, if it be not submissive to the Divinity?[41]

Had Dawkins taken the trouble to read any of de Tocqueville's writings about the United States, he would not be so puzzled and perplexed by America's religious affinities nor so unschooled on the historical facts of the influence of Christian thinking on the American forefathers. Dawkins wisely does not take his "dechristianization" of American history beyond the generation of the founders. Hitchens, on the other hand, has no such compunction, determined as he is to prove that religious motivations could not be the reason for any decent human behavior or the accomplishments of any age or any culture.

Hitchens takes on Abraham Lincoln, whom he briskly dismisses as "a tormented skeptic with a tendency to deism."[42] In this, he is only partially correct. It is true that Lincoln, both before and during his presidency, never formally joined any church and was careful to eschew closely identifying with any Christian denomination. But where Hitchens errs is in ascribing deistic beliefs to Lincoln. It becomes increasingly apparent reading through *God Is Not Great* that Hitchens simply doesn't understand what deism is. Above all, deists believe that God, having set everything in the universe in motion, no longer involves himself in human activities. Lincoln, however, in his private conversations with friends clearly revealed a belief in God's intervening hand in the affairs of humankind—a direct contradiction of the central belief of deism. "I am conscious every moment," he told biographer J. A. Reed, "that all I am and all I have is subject to the control of a Higher Power, and that Power can use me or not use me in any manner, and at any time, as in His wisdom and might may be pleasing to Him."[43]

Lincoln's March 1863 "Proclamation Appointing a National Fast Day," in which he alludes to the Civil War as possibly being divine judgment meted out on America for the sin of slavery, opens with these words: "Whereas, the Senate of the United States, devoutly recognizing the Supreme Authority and just Government of Almighty God, in all the affairs of men and of nations, has, by a resolution, requested the President to designate and set apart a day for National prayer and humiliation. . . ." The proclamation continues, "But we have forgotten God. We have forgotten the gracious hand which preserved us in peace, and multiplied and enriched and strengthened us. . . ."[44]

Lincoln was forthright about his seeming lack of piety, and indeed never hid the fact that he was not a member of any church. He told a group of Presbyterians in Baltimore, "I have often wished that I was a more devout man than I am; nevertheless, amid the greatest difficulties of my administration, when I could not see any other resort, I would place my whole reliance in God, knowing that all would go well, and that He would decide for the right."[45] In fact, as president, Lincoln regularly attended services at Washington's New York Avenue Presbyterian Church. He did not, however, sit prominently in a pew. Rather, he stood out of sight of the main congregation, in the study of the pastor, Dr. Phineas Gurley.

According to Gurley, Lincoln became a Christian as a result not only of the loss of his twelve-year-old son, Willy, in 1862, but also of the shock of surveying the carnage after the July 1863 Battle of Gettysburg. The veracity of Gurley's and several others' accounts of Lincoln's conversion continues to be debated to this day, and Lincoln's precise spiritual worldview may never be entirely known. What is clear, though, is that the crushing weight of the responsibility of holding the country together during the Civil War created in Lincoln a profound awareness of the puniness of man and the omnipotence, even inscrutability, of God.

Lincoln was not alone among American presidents to admit that the seemingly insuperable challenges of the office had forced him to his knees. Even in the decidedly more secular atmosphere of recent decades, modern American presidents have acknowledged the need for prayer when all else failed. President George W. Bush has repeatedly told audiences how invaluable he finds their prayers. "I want to tell you," he said in a May 2002 address to the National Hispanic Prayer Breakfast, "the greatest gift that people can give to a President or people in positions of responsibility—anybody else, for that matter—is prayer."[46]

Throughout almost the entirety of the two-hundred-plus-year history of the United States, Americans have regarded their country as an "exceptional" nation; the notion that America's destiny was set even before the nation was formally established seems embedded in the national genes. That belief has not spared the United States suffering, anguish, even humiliation in its journey through history. Sometimes, the country has seemed triumphalist and conceited in its religiosity, a characteristic that has surely irritated, if not alarmed, older nations—especially in Europe, which in many ways seems on a permanent slide down a slope toward religionless skepticism. Europeans, particularly those in the media,[47] have tended to roll their eyes whenever American political leaders invoke the Almighty as part of serious national discourse. Whatever the response of non-Americans may be, however, the religious flavor of American life can be said to be a constant in the American *way* of life, though its manifestations may ebb and flow. Significant numbers of Americans believe that that constancy, while not sparing the nation from its tragedies and humiliations, *has* protected it from the most extremist behaviors and conflicts that can plague such a multicultural society.

Beyond American shores, the debate that is endemic to world politics and culture is which worldview—whether entirely secular or religious, and if religious, representing what religion—should govern the philosophy of nations. A life-and-death struggle is being waged in many parts of the world between moderate and extremely radical interpretations of Islamic belief. If the radical side prevails, the result will be massive social upheavals, women barred from education, freedom of thought and expression prohibited, much medical and scientific research halted, and the death penalty meted out for the "crime" of not being a Muslim.

In other parts of the world—South Asia, for example—religious radicalism has taken the form of attempting to peel back the layers of religious pluralism brought by European colonial powers. These colonial powers had laid upon the cultures of India, Pakistan, Bangladesh, and Sri Lanka the Western ideals of freedom of thought and of religion, but these ideals are now being linked to the humiliation of forced submission to the European conquerors and are being repudiated.

In still other places, where deliberately atheist Communist regimes have wreaked suffering and chaos on national life, it is the secular rationalism of the atheist worldview that is being challenged. Nowhere is that more apparent than in China, the sole remaining world power still ruled by the Communist Party. The collapse of Chairman Mao Tse-tung's radical collectivist totalitarianism that prevailed from 1949 to 1976 has been followed in the past twenty-five years by welcome encouragement of free enterprise and widely enhanced personal freedoms. At the same time, however, widespread dishonesty throughout society and massive corruption at all levels of government and business (want to buy "made in China" toys or pet food with ingredients imported from China?) has proved to be an intractable problem for the Chinese government because it can't find a way to make its citizens behave virtuously. The Beijing leadership can't adopt the solution of the American Founding Fathers—the three-legged stool of religion, virtue, and freedom—because that would have the unintended consequence of encouraging religious belief, which in turn would directly undermine the legitimacy of the Communists to rule. That legitimacy, of course, is based on the fiction that Marx discovered the ironclad laws of history and that the Chinese Communist Party is heir to the interpretation of those laws.

Only a tiny minority of Chinese still believe in orthodox Marxism-Leninism, that is, that under the dictatorship of the proletariat—the Communist Party—Chinese society is transitioning through socialism toward the nirvana of Communism, that future ideal Marxist polity where the state has withered away. The Chinese have lost faith in Marxism-Leninism not simply because it patently hasn't worked—China's prosperity today has come from embracing capitalism—but because this Marxist philosophy, chained to the iron ball of state atheism, has left it in a moral wasteland.

It is perhaps not at all surprising, therefore, that Christianity is now not only the fastest-growing religion in China, but is already approaching critical mass. That is, if the current growth trend continues, the numbers of Chinese who are Christian, now estimated at between 8 percent and 13 percent of the population, could reach 25 percent; that would make China essentially a Christianized nation.[48] If the majority of the American intelligentsia has forgotten America's origins, not as a "Christian" nation but as one accountable—in the Old Testament sense—to God, many Chinese scholars are newly discovering that fact. When a group of eighteen American tourists were in Beijing in 2002 on a tour of the landmarks of Western missionary efforts in China, they met with a scholar from the Chinese Academy of Social Sciences, the nation's most prestigious academic institute in the fields of philosophy and social sciences. What the scholar had to say astonished them:

> One of the things we were asked to look into was what accounted for the success, in fact, the preeminence of the

West all over the world. We studied everything we could from the historical, political, economic, and cultural perspective. At first, we thought it was because you had the best political system. Next we focused on your economic system. But in the past twenty years, we have realized that the heart of your culture is your religion: Christianity. That is why the West has been so powerful. The Christian moral foundation of social and cultural life was what made possible the emergence of capitalism and then the successful transition to democratic politics. We don't have any doubt about this.[49]

In time, China may stop arresting Christian preachers and may become democratic. If so, the Communist Party will lose its monopoly on political power and will become one party among many in China. But whoever leads China will still be faced with the same challenges, the same question of how to raise up a citizenry virtuous enough to make a democratic republic work: How do you make citizens *virtuous* enough to sustain freedom?

A young Chinese journalist, totally educated in the atheist education system of Communist China, in September 2007 presented a paper at an academic conference in Chicago recounting his two-year personal search for the answer to that very question. In his paper entitled "God and the Essence of Liberty: A Preliminary Inquiry into the History of Freedom," thirty-one-year-old Hong Xu's conclusion couldn't be more clear: "The single most important thing I would like to share with you here is this . . . faith in God as Lord is the beginning of freedom." He explained how he came to this understanding:

> The more I knew about the growth of freedom in the West, the more I was captivated by the role of faith in God as Lord in the making of a free and responsible civilization. . . .
>
> A major reason for the stillbirth of freedom in non-Western societies is that the bedrock for the building of liberty was missing in these cultures. That is, faith in God as Lord did not become the vital part of the non-Western consciousness. One cannot say that individuals in those parts of the world did not want freedom. Yet in societies like China, with which I'm most familiar, freedom could not stand a realistic chance of becoming a positive value or a viable institution in much of their history because rule by men instead of the rule of law was the constant pattern. For them, law was virtually the will of the men in power. . . .
>
> Without faith in God as Lord, freedom—with the popular (mis)conception of doing anything one wants—could only be perceived by anyone in power as a threat to the established order. However, for societies where faith in God as Lord figures prominently, law is independent of the will of humans. It's the will of God, the Lord. The only truly right thing one can do is to do the divine will.[50]

Xu, who has adopted the English name "Promise," is not alone in his conclusions. The prominent young mainland Chinese dissident writer Yu Jie told me over dinner in August 2007 that Chinese intellectuals view with irony the New Atheist books that have made such a splash in the United States. The irony derives from the fact that at this very moment in China, scholars, intellectuals, and other thoughtful members of Chinese society are increasingly curious about Christianity, and many are seeing the benefits of Christian values to underpin and hold together a society buffeted by social, moral, and political challenges. A Chinese psychiatrist who was an active participant in the historic 1989 Tiananmen Square pro-democracy movement that was brutally suppressed by the army wrote a short essay in July 2007 in which he noted the burst of interest in the New Atheism books by the Four Horsemen. He countered their views, writing, "When people believe there's a God and heaven and hell and judgment, then they will not dare to brazenly do wrong, [rather] they will try their utmost to do what is right. When people live a Christian life, they will have hearts of justice and love, hearts that willingly and happily act with justice and love."[51]

Perhaps even more startling is a commentary that appeared in the *Beijing Evening News*, a government-controlled newspaper, in February 2007, in which the writer lamented, "In recent years, the lack of faith and core values has brought us pain and suffering: we've seen too much corruption, cold-bloodedness and cheating; we can't trust anyone; we can't buy a single food item without worry . . . in sum, nothing can be trusted, every-thing is risky." He continued,

> Some may ask, in Western society, where secularism also stands as the dominant mainstream [influence], how do people resolve the problem of spiritual belonging? Let me just point out two simple facts here: 1) the spiritual pain and suffering that Western societies went through was just as serious [as ours is now]; 2) compared with the East, the West has its own distinctive religious tradition. As [German political economist and sociologist Max] Weber pointed out, "From the perspective of the Protestant [believer], the success of worldly economic activity is not in the creation of wealth to be enjoyed and squandered, rather it is to confirm the grace and favor one receives from God"—this is the very [mechanism that] . . . constrains immoral behavior.[52]

The Founding Fathers understood that atheism was the worst possible worldview a society could adopt. Chinese raised on a lifelong diet of atheism and living in an entirely atheistic world are increasingly coming to the same conclusion. Perhaps the New Atheists should look to the Chinese for instruction. They might learn a thing or two.

# THE
# NEW ATHEISM
## OFFERS NOTHING NEW

*Dawkins: "There could be something incredibly grand and*
*incomprehensible and beyond our present understanding."*
*Collins: "That's God. . . ."*[1]
From *Time* magazine debate between Richard Dawkins,
and Francis Collins, director of the National Human Genome
Research Institute (NHGRI), September 30, 2006

Much of what the New Atheists have written is not new; atheists have come and gone throughout history. Richard Dawkins, Daniel Dennett, Sam Harris, and Christopher Hitchens are but the latest in a long line of vocal and vociferous anti-God thinkers and writers spanning the centuries and the world. Among Indian religions, some streams of Hinduism have been atheistic, and Buddhism—depending on what kind of Buddhism it is—can be explicitly atheistic. In the West, atheism had its roots among Greek philosophers before the time of Socrates (ca. 470–399 BC), and also had exponents in the persons of Democritus (ca. 460–ca. 370 BC) and Epicurus (341–270 BC). The Roman writer Lucretius (ca. 99–ca. 55 BC) was another materialist who was entirely skeptical of the existence of the divine, preceding Hitchens's moan about "how religion poisons everything" by a couple of millennia with his much-quoted dictum, "*Tantum religio potuit suadere malorum*" (So much evil has religion wrought). During the Renaissance, the Italian philosopher, priest, and occultist Giordano Bruno (1548–1600) speculated about an infinite universe and was ultimately tried and burned at the stake as a heretic, earning him the title of "the first martyr for science." Fortunately for everyone, not long afterward the Catholic Church stopped burning heretics. Of course, the atheists themselves, once they held the reins of government, acted out far more vicious persecutions of religious believers than the empowered church had ever used against atheists, as we saw in chapter 5.

Although England was the birthplace of deism in the seventeenth century, it was to France that the center of a radical critique of Christianity and of general belief in God later moved. During the French Enlightenment, French *philosophes* such as Denis Diderot (1713–1784) and Paul-Henri Thiry, baron d'Holbach (1723–1789), and skeptics such as Thomas Paine in the United States carried the torch of radical anti-Christianity as far as they could take it. The famed French Enlightenment writer Voltaire was a deist and not an atheist, but his animosity toward the Christian church is well known. For instance, he called Christianity "the most ridiculous, the most absurd and bloody religion that has ever infected the world."[2] In England, the deist Thomas Woolston (1669–1731) predicted that Christianity would die out by the year 1900.

A long procession of anti-God writers emerged in the nineteenth and twentieth centuries: German philosopher Ludwig Andreas Feuerbach; "father of communism" Karl Marx; one of the "fathers of modern anarchism," Mikhail Alexandrovich Bakunin; Marx's coauthor Friedrich Engels; Scottish philosopher David Hume; American freethought orator Robert G. Ingersoll; philosopher and 1950 Nobel laureate in literature Bertrand Russell; "father of psychoanalysis" Sigmund Freud; French author and philosopher Albert Camus; French existentialist philosopher Jean-Paul Sartre; and Antony Flew, the British philosopher whose conversion from atheism to deism in 2004, at the age of eighty-one, grabbed headlines.

These are just a few of the glittering personalities in the pantheon of atheistic thinkers. At the end of the nineteenth century, Friedrich Nietzsche announced that "God is dead," and furthermore that Europeans had killed him. Nietzsche has acquired a malevolent reputation because of the influence his thought had on Hitler, the Nazis, and more recently on the "deconstructionists,"—that is, philosophers who maintain that the only ultimate reality is power and that all truths are relative. A few others in the list of prominent atheist writers and thinkers have evil reputations too, notably the Marquis de Sade, Annie Besant, Edward Aveling, and Madalyn Murray O'Hair. These atheists led deeply amoral lives, and their atheist worldview caused them in many instances to act with profound malevolence toward others.

Annie Besant (1847–1933) was something of an archetypical hitchhiker through the anti-God universe, picking up and discarding beliefs with the same frequency with which she took on new lovers. Through romances with the world-renowned Irish writer George Bernard Shaw and English Marxist Edward Aveling, she moved from plain old secularism to Marxism to Fabian socialism and then to Theosophy, which is a view of the world that combines spiritism, clairvoyance, and elements of Hindu and Buddhist mysticism. Besant, in effect, was "converted" from atheism to an esoteric form of oriental occultism. Her onetime lover Aveling was such an unprincipled rogue that even the Marxists disowned him after he manipulated his longtime lover, Eleanor Marx, the daughter of Karl Marx, into taking her own life.

Late in the twentieth century, another particularly unsavory atheist made an appearance: Madalyn Murray O'Hair (1919–1995). She was an atheist with whom Americans should be familiar and about whom American atheists ought to be excruciatingly embarrassed. She founded American Atheists after achieving national prominence when her lawsuit resulted in the 1963 U.S. Supreme Court ban on officially sponsored prayer in public schools. The suit was brought on behalf of her son William J. Murray who, she said, was being forced to attend Bible readings in school and was being harassed for resisting. Ironically, this son announced in 1980 that he had become a born-again Christian. He was baptized in Gateway Baptist Church in Dallas, Texas, and wrote a book about his experiences growing up in the home of the most famous American atheist. O'Hair disowned him with this ugly public denunciation, "One could call this a postnatal abortion on the part of a mother, I guess; I repudiate him entirely and completely for now and all times. . . . He is beyond human forgiveness."[3]

As this statement demonstrates, O'Hair was an exceptionally hateful person who made no attempt to conceal her anger and hostility toward anyone who opposed her or whose views she found distasteful. Murray wrote that he was "taught that because there was no God there was no such thing as right or wrong. My mother told me it was better to be a homosexual than to be a Christian. She taught me that the most important things in life were the physical pleasures of drink, food and sex."[4] O'Hair did not just confine her abuse to Christians or other theists. She was venomous toward homosexuals and responded with obscene and abusive letters to them when they asked for help. She also allegedly stole money from American Atheists that she stashed in accounts all over the world.

The full account of O'Hair's actions at American Atheists may never be known. She disappeared in 1995, along with her other son, Jon Garth Murray, and her granddaughter, Robin Murray O'Hair, the daughter of William, setting off rumors that O'Hair had simply fled with funds from the organization. Fueling the speculation was the fact that shortly after they disappeared, Jon Murray received $500,000 worth of coins from a San Antonio jeweler. Ultimately, a disgruntled former employee of American Atheists, David Roland Waters, was charged with kidnapping and murdering the trio, whose bodies were uncovered in 2001 after Waters told police exactly where to look. They had been sawn into pieces and mutilated. Waters had a criminal record before O'Hair hired him and apparently began stealing from the organization even while he was an employee.

Brian Lynch, the former treasurer of American Atheists, whom Madalyn fired after accusing him of sexual misconduct (which he emphatically denied), has said, "When you mention atheism to most people, the only name they can think of is Madalyn Murray O'Hair, a loudmouth who had a bad family life, communist ideas, and a negative personality. She's brought atheism into a position of intellectual disrepute, accomplishing in twenty-five years what churches haven't been able to accomplish in centuries. I think she ought to get a check from the Pope."[5]

But Madalyn Murray O'Hair was by no means the first to give atheism a bad name. Even before the French Revolution of 1789 demonstrated the wickedness that atheists in power can inflict against people of faith, the century's most notorious exponent of atheism was already on the scene: the Marquis de Sade (1740–1814), whose name is the root for the word *sadism*. De Sade was a lustful sexual predator with a taste for physical violence as part of his sexual pleasure. He physically abused prostitutes and other women repeatedly, and spent much of his life in prisons and insane asylums, where he continued to write about his ideas advocating total sexual freedom. In de Sade's 1782 work, *Dialogue between a Priest and a Dying Man*,[6] written while in prison, the dying libertine says to the priest, "Your god is a machine you fabricated to serve your passions; you manipulated it so that it suited them—but the moment it interfered with mine, I kicked it out of my way, and was glad to do so." In a 1795 work, *Philosophy in the Bedroom*, de Sade describes a fifteen-year-old nun who has abandoned faith in God as she discovers the delights of sodomy, incest, and flagellation.[7] "The idea of God," writes the theologian and Oxford professor Alister McGrath in his interesting book *The Twilight of Atheism: The Rise and Fall of Disbelief in the Modern World*, "is firmly presented, as an outmoded superstition that merely gets in the way of enjoying life to the full . . . the link was clear: atheism made sexual experimentation legitimate and interesting."[8]

A link has indeed existed throughout modern history between conscious rejection of moral restraint and atheism. Some atheists have privately admitted that their vociferous rejection of God was a way to justify a completely libertine and immoral lifestyle. In an article entitled "Confession of a Professed Atheist," the novelist Aldous Huxley (1894–1963), best known for his novel *Brave New World*, explained:

> For myself, as no doubt for most of my friends, the philosophy of meaninglessness was essentially an instrument of

liberation from a certain system of morality. We objected to the morality because it interfered with our sexual freedom. The supporters of this system claimed that it embodied the meaning—the Christian meaning, they insisted—of the world. There was one admirably simple method of confuting these people and justifying ourselves in our erotic revolt: we would deny that the world had any meaning whatever.[9]

Huxley followed the same trail from atheism into meaninglessness that Annie Besant had followed. Not only did he become an adherent of Indian mysticism, he also started taking the peyote-derived drug mescaline and the psychedelic drug LSD. As he lay dying on November 22, 1963 (the same day that John F. Kennedy and the Christian apologist C. S. Lewis both died), he was injected, at his request, with one final dose of LSD.

According to McGrath, world atheism peaked in the two-hundred-year period between the outbreak of the French Revolution in 1789 and the collapse of Communism in 1989. At the apogee of this period, around 1960, as much as half the world's population might have been at least nominally atheist. McGrath concludes, "With Stalin and Madalyn Murray O'Hair, atheism seems to have ended up by mimicking the vices of the Spanish Inquisition and the worst televangelists, respectively. Yet this is not to say anything especially negative about atheism—merely that it is just as prone as any other system of thought to the frailties and failing of human nature. Far from being a solution to the human dilemma, it has become part of the problem."[10]

That is precisely the point. Atheists individually are as prone to human vices as religious believers; they are, after all, part of the human condition. To claim that "religion poisons everything," as Hitchens does in *God Is Not Great*, is to imply that people who lack religious faith may somehow be immune from the poisons of vice, crime, cruelty, and folly. But this is manifestly not the case. This is not to say that atheists are worse in their behavior, on average, than people of religious faith. Obviously that is not so; as I have already noted, individual atheists have been, and are, capable of exemplary behavior. It is when atheism is adopted as an exclusive worldview by people holding political power that real crimes are often committed, as we recounted in chapter 5. The reason for this is that atheists in power hold humankind to be the ultimate source of moral authority. Human beings, in the view of atheists, are at the center of the universe and are not just the ultimate judges of their own behavior but also the ones who decide—quite arbitrarily—what the standards are for good and evil.

In fact, the qualities of good and evil seem to present serious moral dilemmas to committed atheists. When presented with exemplary embodiments of altruistic behavior, such as Mother Teresa, Richard Dawkins retreats behind Hitchens's excoriation of her in his book *The Missionary Position*. Hitchens, of course, stands by his determination to mock and dispute all saintly behavior attributed to Christians. He even refuses to acknowledge that Christian convictions may have been behind Martin Luther King Jr.'s heroic efforts to advance the cause of civil rights for African Americans. He apparently doesn't believe—in the face of overwhelming evidence to the contrary—that Dietrich Bonhoeffer, murdered by the Nazis, was a genuine Christian. In contradiction to his overall thesis that "religion poisons everything," Hitchens nevertheless grudgingly admits that Christians may be playing a positive role in drawing the world's attention to the human rights crisis in Darfur, Sudan, and in opposing the vicious totalitarian dictatorship of North Korea's tyrant Kim Il Sung. He doesn't, of course, explain how that faith-based motivation squares with his thesis that "religion poisons everything."

All Four Horsemen purport to believe that there is an evolutionary kink in the human DNA that has created some kind of instinctive "solidarity" among humans. They don't explain how it works—in fact, they themselves apparently are *unable* to explain how it works—but they seem convinced that it is there. The real challenge for atheism, however, is not in explaining why occasionally people do great acts of goodness, but rather why some people commit acts of unmitigated evil. Leaving aside the issue of whether Hitler was a Catholic or how genuine Kim Il Sung or Pol Pot's atheism was, a commonsense, man-on-the-street understanding seems to exist worldwide that some deeds are just plain evil. People of faith and of no faith *do* seem to share the following beliefs: The Holocaust was evil, Stalin's incarceration of millions in the *gulag* was evil, Pol Pot's genocidal social engineering was evil, and the September 11 terrorist attacks on the World Trade Center and the Pentagon were evil.

But what exactly does "evil" mean to an atheist? The Four Horsemen seem to have no compunction about describing certain human behavior as "immoral" even though they can't point to any agreed-upon way of defining the term. In recent decades, conventional psychiatry and sociology have tended to discourage using the word *evil* to describe bad actions. This led to the folly taught by some child-rearing literature to call children's behavior "inappropriate" rather than "bad."[11] "Bad," after all, implies some moral judgment. Dawkins, in fact, seems still to be living in this twilight zone of unreality. In the *Time* debate excerpted at the beginning of this chapter, Dawkins and Francis Collins have this exchange:

> Collins: What you've said implies that outside of the human mind, tuned by evolutionary processes, good and evil have no meaning. Do you agree with that?
>
> Dawkins: Even the question you're asking has no meaning to me. Good and evil—I don't believe that there is hanging out there, anywhere, something called good and something called evil. I think that there are good things that happen and bad things that happen.[12]

The kindest thing that can be said about Dawkins's statement here is that it reveals an astonishing poverty of moral imagination. Even Harris and Hitchens seem to shy away from that degree of moral agnosticism. Again, aside from the issue of what philosophical beliefs or nonbeliefs men like Hitler and Stalin embraced, where are the resources of moral outrage needed to cope with events such as the Holocaust or the Great Purges in the Soviet Union in the 1930s or Pol Pot's Killing Fields? In the face of evil so monstrous that the mind reels in grasping for adjectives adequate to describe it, atheism seems to respond with a fatuous philosophical version of "please call back during normal business hours." Yet if atheism itself can't agree on criteria for defining actions or people as good or evil, can atheists explain why there seems to be a universal human need do so? Even if, like Dawkins, an atheist doesn't want to use those morally qualifying terms, what kink of evolution seems to make some people behave much, much worse than the mere perpetuation of one's genes would require?

Another, more revealing side to this poverty of moral imagination comes through in all the books by the New Atheists. Among the Four Horsemen, only Dennett concedes that something remarkable might exist in the fervor of people who are committed to a personal faith, and only Harris admits that a hunger for, as well as real contact with, the transcendent might exist in the human experience.[13] The tapestry of human behavior throughout all cultures and all ages of human history is almost incomprehensibly rich and colorful. The range of experiences and feelings within it is as limitless as the human condition itself is broad. Yet the New Atheists seem utterly oblivious, even purposefully inattentive, to any intimation of the divine, any human transformation in the presence of God as attested to by millions and millions of people. The atheists seem as tone-deaf to moral reality as deaf students on a field trip to a performance of Beethoven's *Ninth Symphony.*

Consider just a few simple examples. There are surely few people alive in the world who have never encountered a friend, a relative, perhaps even a stranger, who has spoken to them about a personal religious experience. Certainly in the United States, this religion-soaked nation which Dawkins seems perversely unable—or unwilling—to comprehend, virtually everyone at some time or other has met a "born-again Christian." To be sure, the encounters with such people are not always trouble free. "Born-agains" can be insensitive, loud, intolerant, arrogant, and many other inappropriate things. But that doesn't nullify the fact that born-agains all seem to have experienced *something* profoundly powerful in their lives. That *something* may have been a deeply emotional experience, or it may have been so subtle that they themselves cannot quite describe it. The famed evangelist Billy Graham once made this observation, based on his more than seven decades of preaching the Christian message the world over: "All over the world people have a difference in the way they react and respond, but not to the Gospel. When the Gospel of Jesus Christ is proclaimed, I just cannot see any difference. Anywhere in the world, whether it's Africa, Asia, or Europe or a university group or a primitive tribe."[14]

Regardless of the terminology—whether it's called the "evangelical moment," "conversion," "regeneration," "coming to faith," or something else in religions other than Christianity—the fact is, millions of people live among us whose exemplary personal behavior is clearly rooted in a religious source. It may be attributable to a personal faith in Christianity's Jesus, or a profound devotion to Judaism's Almighty. (I do not exclude the possibility of exemplary moral behavior inspired by Islam or other religious belief systems; I simply haven't encountered it myself.) Whether it be the selfless care given to a disabled family member, the sacrifice of personal time to mentor or coach a child from an impoverished background, or a teenager's decision to spend his summer building simple homes in a foreign country, the instances of acts of human kindness unmistakably founded on faith-based motivations are so numerous they could fill a whole library.

Even more striking are the wasted and wicked lives that have been turned around through unquestionably profound personal religious experiences. *The Cross and the Switchblade* tells just such stories about young, drug-addicted gang members in New York City whose lives were transformed by a small-town pastor from Pennsylvania who went to the dark streets of Manhattan and Brooklyn in 1959 to try to help them. David Wilkerson has been transforming lives ever since, and his drug recovery program now spans the world. Jackie Pullinger has effected similar transformations in Hong Kong. A British missionary there since the late 1960s, she has led a life of service to the outcasts of Hong Kong society—heroin addicts, secret society enforcers, beggars, aging prostitutes, and the like. I became close friends with Jackie when I was living in Hong Kong in the 1970s. I have seen her at work, and I have met some of the people she has helped. Jackie's phenomenal success rests on bringing, through personal faith in Jesus Christ, a source of power into these people's lives that can dramatically turn them around.

Wilkerson and Pullinger are but two examples from the extraordinarily rich literature throughout the past two millennia of Christian history that testify to the transforming power of personal Christian faith. The testimony of millions upon millions of people worldwide to that very same transformation stands as a rebuke to the shallow generalizations of the New Atheists. One way of putting it is that while the Four Horsemen's historical observations and generalizations *do* describe a portion of life, to suggest that their view reflects the totality of the experiences of most people most of the time insults the human intelligence. Those people who deny that such remarkable altruistic individuals exist or deny the experience that motivated or even changed such individuals live in a two-dimensional universe.

In fact, the world in which we all live today owes its greatest attributes to Christianity. That may at first seem an extreme claim. Historical facts, however, show that our modern age with its science and technology, its medicine, its law courts and universities, its global commerce, its free flow of information (with the striking exception of China and the handful of other communist—and therefore atheist—countries) would simply not exist but for the systematic embrace, century after century, of a Christian view of life.

The common understanding about the spread of early Christianity is that the Roman Empire, after feeding some Christians to hungry lions over the course of a few decades, became Christian overnight in 313, when the emperor Constantine issued the Edict of Toleration in Milan. According to this account, Christianity then spread instantly throughout the former Roman Empire until Rome itself fell in 476, whereupon Europe entered the Dark Ages, only to reemerge some six hundred years later in early medieval times.

The truth is actually very different, and quite sobering. From the reign of the emperor Augustus (63 BC–AD 14) onward, the Roman Empire was held together by its invincible armies, an excellent system of law and administration, superbly engineered Roman roads and pirate-free navigation throughout the Mediterranean world, and a sense of imperial destiny to civilize the areas conquered by the Roman armies. Following Rome's collapse in the fifth century, however, barbarian armies who had migrated westward from modern-day Eastern Europe overran the former Roman Empire. Some of these invading tribes had been Christianized; many had not. Just about everyone was illiterate. The only centers of civilization where classical learning was preserved were the Christian monasteries, standing like so many lonely lighthouses shining over a sea of civilizational darkness. Writer and historian Thomas Cahill has done an immense service to our understanding of this period by describing in his book *How the Irish Saved Civilization* exactly how precarious learning, scholarship, and culture were in Europe from the fall of Rome to the rise of the emperor Charlemagne. What kept it all alive, kept all these treasures of civilization from being swallowed up by barbarism and ignorance, were these little outposts of Christian community, first in Ireland, then in Anglo-Saxon England, and finally throughout the continent of Europe.

Armed conquest played some role in the spread of Christianity northward in the next few centuries, but it was minimal. It took centuries of tireless, heroic Christian missionary endeavors to extend Christendom to the northern vastness of Europe. Iceland was not Christianized until AD 1000 and Norway not until about 1007. It was the courageous Anglo-Saxon Boniface (672–754), a Benedictine monk who was sent as a missionary to the Frankish empire, who brought Christianity to the warlike, barbarian, and superstitious Germans. In the year AD 723, Boniface took an ax to the sacred oak tree of Thor, in the modern-day western-central German state of Hesse, challenging the pagan god—if he existed—to strike him down. The oak tree fell, Boniface lived—for thirty-one more years. And Europe took a turn that changed its history forever: It turned away from superstition and adopted Christianity.

That conversion was not just a switch of spiritual allegiance:

from gods who lived in trees and so forth to a God who had led the Hebrews out of Egypt and who sent to the world the Christian Savior. Rather, the change was a profound and systematic transformation of patterns of thought. There was a place specifically reserved for reason and the unhampered judgment of the free intellect. That pattern of thinking—albeit with some zigzags in its development—eventually came to dominate the culture of Europe. Thence it spread to North America. Eventually, the use of reason and the development of science conquered the whole world.

Nine years after Boniface felled the pagan oak tree, his Frankish protector Charles Martel, better known in modern English as Charles the Hammer, defeated the invading Arabs at Tours, France, thus saving Europe from falling into the domain of Islam. If the Muslims had not been turned back at that point, Western civilization would have taken a dramatically different road and our world today would be quite different from what it is. As noted in the previous chapter, a world dominated by radical Islam would be one in which none of the freedoms that have characterized the history of the West would exist at all.

No historian has captured the significance of Christianity in civilizing Europe and indeed the whole of the West better than the late Christopher Dawson (1889–1970), the English scholar and writer of cultural history and Christianity. In his brilliant summation of this achievement in *Religion and the Rise of Western Culture*, Dawson wrote:

Why is it that Europe alone among the civilizations of the world has been continually shaken and transformed by an energy of spiritual unrest that refuses to be content with the unchanging law of social tradition which rules oriental cultures? It is because its religious ideal has not been the worship of timeless and changeless perfection but a spirit that strives to incorporate itself in humanity and to change the world. In the West the spiritual power has not been immobilized in a sacred social order like the Confucian state in China and the Indian caste system. It has acquired social freedom and autonomy and consequently its activity has not been confined to the religious sphere but has had far-reaching effects on every aspect of social and intellectual life. . . .

The more one studies the origins of humanism, the more one is brought to recognize the existence of an element which is not only spiritual but definitely Christian.[15]

Modern sociologists have come to identical conclusions. Rodney Stark, the American sociologist of religion, picks up essentially where Dawson leaves off in two important books, *For the Glory of God: How Monotheism Led to Reformations, Science, Witch-hunts, and the End of Slavery* and *The Victory of Reason: How Christianity Led to Freedom, Capitalism, and Western Success*. Stark's point is that from medieval times onward, Christianity stressed the vital connection of reason with the Christian faith, in fact emphasized a *faith* in reason:

During the past century Western intellectuals have been more than willing to trace European imperialism to Christian origins, but they have been entirely unwilling to recognize that Christianity made any contribution (other than intolerance) to the Western capacity to dominate. Rather, the West is said to have surged ahead precisely as it *overcame* religious barriers to progress, especially those impeding science. Nonsense. The success of the West, including the rise of science, rested entirely on religious foundations, and the people who brought it about were devout Christians. (emphasis in the original)[16]

In a manner emphasized by scientists and mathematicians as varied as the English-born mathematician-turned-philosopher Alfred North Whitehead and the American theoretical physicist J. Robert Oppenheimer, Christianity erected the engine room for modern science by insisting that the universe was orderly in structure, by asserting that God's physical laws were open to investigation, and by expressing the belief that God would be glorified in the progressive revelation of them. As Stark writes:

The Christian image of God is that of a rational being who *believes in human progress*, more fully revealing himself as humans *gain* the capacity to better understand. Moreover, because God is a rational being and the universe is his personal creation, it necessarily has a rational, lawful, stable structure *awaiting increased human comprehension*. This was the key to many intellectual undertakings, among them the rise of science. (emphasis in the original)[17]

He continues:

> Christianity created Western Civilization. Had the followers of Jesus remained an obscure Jewish sect, most of you would not have learned to read and the rest of you would be reading from hand-copied scrolls. Without a theology committed to reason, progress and moral equality, today the entire world would be about where non-European societies were in, say, 1800: A world with many astrologers and alchemists but no scientists. A world of despots, lacking universities, banks, factories, eyeglasses, chimneys, and pianos. A world where most infants do not live to the age of five and many women die in childbirth—a world truly living in 'dark ages.' . . .
>
> There are many reasons people embrace Christianity, including its capacity to sustain a deeply emotional and existentially satisfying faith. But another significant factor is its appeal to reason and the fact that it is so inseparably linked to the rise of Western Civilization. For many non-Europeans, becoming a Christian is intrinsic to becoming modern.[18]

Christianity, of course, gave rise to modern atheism, and developed the conditions where the autonomy of reason could be used as a tool to demolish not just Christianity and all faiths, but reason itself. But what a dismal world we should all live in if the New Atheists succeed in persuading a majority of the population of the world that they were right. It would be a world where the instruction of children in religious thought, if Dawkins has his way, would be considered "child abuse" (as it was in the Soviet Union, many Eastern European communist countries, and China) and children would be removed from the care of religious parents. It would be a world in which the composer Bach, the painter Tintoretto, and the writers Milton and Dostoevsky might well be considered "cultural" giants by Hitchens, but studying their works from the perspective of what they believed (because they were religious) would not be allowed—a world in which, if Harris had his way, people with ideas that he considered "dangerous" would be done away with entirely. It would be a world where political power is the determinant of truth and of what is moral or immoral. It would be a world of such desperate moral emptiness that those who believe in the Second Coming of Christ would pray daily, even hourly for that great day to arrive.

But there is another possibility: that of science and religion not battering each other, as Dawkins seems to think is always inevitable, but enriching each other deeply. "Science is the only reliable way to understand the natural world," says Francis Collins, director of the National Human Genome Research Institute and discoverer of many genetic sequences that lead to specific diseases, "and its tools when properly utilized can generate profound insights into material existence. But," he adds, "science is powerless to answer questions such as 'Why did the universe come into being?' 'What is the meaning of human existence?' 'What happens after we die?' One of the strongest motivations of humankind is to seek answers to profound questions, and we need to bring all the power of both scientific and spiritual perspectives to bear on understanding what is both seen and unseen."[19]

Science, however, is itself vulnerable to variations on the old anti-Christian heresy of gnosticism, the belief that the material world is not real and that spiritual truth is quite separate from the physical laws of the universe. According to this heresy, spiritual truth, moreover, can be revealed only to select initiates who have the special knowledge needed, the *gnosis*. It has been suggested that Greek science went into decline around 200 BC partly because the rise of gnostic mystery cults undermined a belief that science could lead to truth.[20] Thomas Kuhn (1922–1996), a professor of the history of science who developed several notions of the philosophy of science, posited that the real reason scientists prefer a new theory to an old one is not the persuasiveness of the new hypothesis backed by testable evidence, but because the new theory is, well, more *appealing* aesthetically. In other words, scientists no longer investigate material reality as though there is a logical thread connecting old theories and discoveries to new ones, but out of rather arbitrary reasons.[21] In effect, this is an appeal for postmodernism in science, a notion wholly destructive of the scientific endeavor, and indeed, of truth itself.

It was Dawkins's fellow Darwinian evolutionary biologist Stephen Jay Gould (1941–2002) who irritated Dawkins immensely by coining the term "non-overlapping magisterial," by which he meant that religion and science dealt with different issues and should not be considered mutually adversarial. He famously added, "Either half my colleagues are enormously stupid, or else the science of Darwinism is fully compatible with conventional religious beliefs—and equally compatible with atheism, thus proving that the two great realms of nature's factuality and the source of human morality do not strongly overlap."[22] John Polkinghorne, a distinguished Cambridge particle physicist who late in life became an Anglican clergyman, expressed more felicitously, "I think I have good reasons for my beliefs, but I do not for a moment suppose that my atheistic friends are simply stupid not to see it my way." This is a sentiment the reverse of which Dawkins apparently has not taken to heart. "I do believe, however," Polkinghorne went on, "that religious belief can explain more than unbelief can do."[23] Perhaps that's because belief is, well, a far more *intelligent* way of looking at the universe than atheism.

And a lot less arrogant.

# THE
# FOUR HORSEMEN
## AND
# THE BIBLE

The Four Horsemen are full of all sorts of denunciations of the Bible, repudiations of both the historical validity of Scripture and of the moral value of both the Hebrew Scriptures and the Christian New Testament. Some Christian readers may feel that this book has failed to address those men's erroneous views of the Bible or counter these attacks. While my approach has not been to defend Christianity but rather to take the offensive against atheism, I realize that I would be remiss if I did not provide some counterbalance to the assertions about the Bible made by Richard Dawkins, Daniel Dennett, Sam Harris, and Christopher Hitchens. It needs to be said that there is no consensus among them on why they distrust the Bible; they contradict both each other and themselves in their fulminations. I am, however, not a trained biblical scholar, and there are others who can do a far better job at explaining where the New Atheists err in their Bible exposition. In fact, in the case of their objections to the New Testament account of Jesus and to the rise of early Christianity, it would require a whole separate book to respond adequately and in detail, and it would require far more expertise in New Testament historical and textual criticism than I have. So this appendix will attempt only to counter a few of the most factually inaccurate claims made by the Four Horsemen.

## *The Ten Commandments*

Richard Dawkins and Sam Harris almost splutter with rage as they tell their readers how reactionary all the Judaic Old Testament commandments are. Christopher Hitchens takes an entirely different approach by saying, in effect, "Don't worry, none of it happened as the Old Testament says it happened anyway, so it doesn't count at all." He does, however, point to the Ten Commandments as an accurate, if historically spurious, way of representing the Old Testament account of God's revelation of himself to the Hebrew people. He argues that it is quite impossible to believe that the Israelites needed to tramp all the way to Mount Sinai in order to grasp that murder, on the whole, was a bad thing. "It is surely insulting to the people of Moses to imagine that they had come this far under the impression that murder, adultery, theft, and perjury were permissible."[1]

Well, it may be "insulting to the people of Moses" (itself a rather bizarre term by which to refer to the ancient Hebrews of the Bible) to suggest that they didn't know murder, theft, and adultery were wrong before Moses lectured them at Mt.

Sinai, but in fact almost all of the people of the ancient world were in a similar bind. The existence of other authoritative legal codes before the Ten Commandments—most notably, the Code of Hammurabi, composed in approximately 1760 BC by Hammurabi, the sixth king of Babylon, and one of the oldest extant legal documents from the ancient Near East—demonstrates that what is right and what is wrong (and that there should be legal penalties for wrongdoing) were not at all universally self-evident in the ancient world. In fact, the consensus of biblical scholars is that the Ten Commandments and other stipulations of the Mosaic law were part of a covenant ratification ceremony that, to a high degree, mimicked what is known about suzerain-vassal treaties describing mutual legal obligations in the ancient Near East. Of course, someone like Hitchens, who denies the existence of God, would dispute the existence of a real "suzerain" in the first place. But what is beyond dispute is the fact that both the ancient and the modern worlds offer up abundant examples of serious moral confusion in situations for which Harris and Hitchens seem to assume that universal human consensus exists about what is right and what is wrong.

Take infanticide, a particularly horrific form of murder. Classical Greece, one of the most admired cultures of the ancient world, had a community that practiced infanticide as a matter of national policy. That community was Sparta, which has a far more laudatory reputation as the Greek state whose soldiers fought so heroically to the last man against the invading Persians at Thermopylae in 480 BC. But in Sparta, any infant who showed the slightest physical imperfection, not to mention deformity, at birth was left out on a hillside to die of exposure. Even worse were the child-sacrifice traditions practiced by many of the pre-Israelite Semitic tribes that inhabited Canaan before the Israelites conquered the land—a practice the ancient Jews found appalling and prohibited entirely. The Phoenicians who settled Carthage engaged in many of these same religious rites of child sacrifice to their god Molech. The Carthaginians also, according to several classical sources, sacrificed their children as part of vows to deities.[2] The Hebrew prophet Jeremiah denounced his fellow Israelites for adopting the child-sacrifice rituals of the Semitic Canaanites whose land the invading Israelites had taken over.[3] The Jewish horror at this practice was confirmed by the historian Josephus (AD 37–ca. 100), who reported that the Jews totally forbade both abortion and infanticide. In the pagan Roman Empire, however, infanticide appears to have been almost routine until it was finally outlawed around AD 374, by which time Rome had essentially been Christianized.

Moreover, the importance and indeed the necessity of the Mosaic injunction against murder has been starkly revealed by the barbarities of "scientific" regimes in the twentieth century. Nazi Germany was the first government to advocate murdering people who were physically deformed or mentally retarded. Not only did the Nazi government advocate this, they were also the first to actually practice it. Once the slippery slope of tolerance of murder is trodden upon, the slide into mass murder and genocide is almost inevitable. What the Nazis tentatively began doing to disabled people at the beginning of Hitler's regime became, by the end of the war, the Holocaust: the wholesale extermination of an entire race.

Tragically, there are intelligent people in respected institutions of learning in the United States who, even today, openly advocate infanticide. Peter Singer, the Australian-born Ira W. DeCamp Professor of Bioethics at Princeton University and a specialist in "practical ethics," is on the record as favoring the murder of infants within thirty days of birth if they are deemed to be severely handicapped. Ironically, Singer is of Jewish background and himself lost family members in the Holocaust.

As for adultery, it is one of the oldest sins in the history of the human race and also one of the most persistent. Hitchens, a journalist, seems unaware that a 1981 poll of 140 leading journalists from elite media organizations found that 54 percent did not think that adultery was wrong, compared with only 15 percent who did.[4] If educated, sophisticated Americans in the late twentieth century have difficulty understanding the immorality of adultery, does Hitchens really believe that the ancient Israelites, on hearing Moses proclaim the seventh commandment against adultery, collectively rolled their eyes and said in unison, "Duh, we knew that already"?

Conservative radio talk-show host Dennis Prager, who is Jewish and has debated Hitchens, puts it succinctly, "The real revolution of the Ten Commandments is that the Creator of the Universe took the time to say certain things were wrong."[5]

## The New Testament

The Four Horsemen are almost as hostile to the New Testament as they are to the Old. Dawkins and Hitchens toy with the idea that Jesus may not have even existed, citing a British scholar, G. A. Wells, who teaches at London University. Wells is not a New Testament specialist at all but a professor of German and a former chairman of the Rationalist Press Association. He has written several books rejecting the historicity of Jesus, a position almost no New Testament scholar endorses, even those who are radically opposed to Christianity. Dawkins appears to be attracted by this theory—after all, if it were true, how much easier it would make his attack upon religion!—but sensibly rejects it in the end. "It is even possible to mount a serious, though not widely supported, historical case that Jesus never lived at all," he says, mentioning in particular Wells and his book, *Did Jesus Exist?* Having suggested that the idea of Jesus' nonexistence is "serious," Dawkins in the next paragraph contradicts himself by saying, "Although Jesus probably existed, reputable biblical scholars do not in general regard the New Testament (and obviously not the Old Testament) as a reliable record of what actually happened in history. . . . "[6]

As stated earlier, a full response to the New Atheists' attacks on the New Testament is beyond the scope of this appendix, and their efforts to debunk the veracity of the New Testament cannot be discussed with the decisive detail that they deserve. Certain dogmatic assertions about the New Testament, however, need to be at least briefly addressed because they are so provocative.

Dawkins, Harris, and Hitchens assert, among other things, that:

1. all the Gospels were written so long after Jesus died that they cannot be considered reliable, and in any case, they contradict each other, especially in regard to the genealogy of Jesus and the Virgin Birth;
2. apart from the point raised above, the Gospels in general are not reliable accounts of what happened;
3. none of the Gospel writers knew Jesus personally, nor are their identities even known;
4. the translation of the Hebrew word *almah* as "virgin" is incorrect (as in "a virgin shall be with child");
5. Jesus never claimed to be divine;
6. the Gospels differ in their accounts of the resurrection of Jesus.

At one level, most of these assertions could be dismissed with the flick of a rhetorical fly whisk: not one of the Four Horsemen seems to have any detailed understanding of either Christianity or of New Testament criticism. Certainly, none of them has any serious background in New Testament scholarship. The only biblical critic cited as an authority for his attempts to debunk the authenticity of the New Testament is Bart Ehrman, chairman of the Department of Religious Studies at the University of North Carolina at Chapel Hill. Ehrman is a former evangelical Christian who lost his faith and now describes himself as an agnostic. His change of heart occurred after his scholarly research revealed that many divergent texts had been incorporated into the New Testament during the historical process of compiling it. Ehrman concluded that the Almighty, if he existed, simply hadn't bothered to ensure an "authentically divine" text. If God couldn't arrange for a "perfect" original text to be preserved, Ehrman says in a number of books with provocative titles (one is called *Misquoting Jesus*), then he probably didn't inspire the writers of Scripture. The problem with Ehrman's thesis is that almost none of the Scriptures he describes as having been inaccurately transmitted are by Jesus at all. Ehrman's critics contend further that not one of the variant textual readings cited by Ehrman has the slightest effect on basic Christian beliefs. Obviously, Ehrman is just the sort of person Dawkins and Hitchens would gravitate to because he starts from the premise that none of Scripture is truthful.

Biblical textual criticism is serious business and requires careful attention to the documents being discussed and an excellent knowledge of their historical and cultural background. The Four Horsemen fall short on both counts. This appendix will take up only a few main points, but a short bibliography is provided of books that address most or all of the assertions at length.

Assertion #1: *All the Gospels were written so long after Jesus died that they cannot be considered reliable, and in any case, they contradict each other, especially in regard to the genealogy of Jesus and the Virgin Birth.* The manuscript evidence for the New Testament is simply huge when compared with other literary works from the ancient world. About 5,000 fragments of the New Testament in Greek and about 10,000 in other ancient languages still exist today. There are fragments of papyrus copies of portions of the Gospels that go back to AD 130. Latin and Coptic copies also go back to the second century, and quotations from the Gospels in the writings of the early church fathers can be dated to around AD 100. There are complete versions of the Gospels, the book of Acts, and Paul's letters dated in the early part of the third century, and complete versions of the book of Revelation from the second half of the third century. Complete volumes of the New Testament date to the early fourth century (i.e., predating the emperor Constantine, who was the first Roman emperor to be a Christian and who *The Da Vinci Code* absurdly asserts created a brand-new version of the New Testament by fiat on the occasion of the Council of Nicaea in AD 325).

By contrast, no more than nine or ten good manuscripts exist of Julius Caesar's *Gallic Wars*, and none dates earlier than nine hundred years after Caesar's chronicling of the nine-year war. None of the books by the Roman historian Tacitus (ca. AD 56–ca. 117) in any form is older than the tenth century AD. As for Aristotle (384–322 BC), not a single manuscript of any of his works dates earlier than AD 1100. Yet no scholar has been rash enough to attack as unreliable these works attributed to Julius Caesar, Tacitus, and Aristotle. Far from working with texts that contradict each other, reputable Bible scholars (although Dawkins would argue that they are not "reputable" because they are not atheists) have concluded that the best text of the Greek New Testament available today is as close to the original documents as it is possible to get. The New Testament scholar F. F. Bruce wrote in his apologetics classic *New Testament Documents: Are They Reliable?* "The variant readings about which any doubt remains among textual critics of the New Testament affect no material question of historic fact or of Christian faith and practice."[7]

The "problem" of the differing genealogies in Matthew and Luke is easily explained: Matthew records the "throne succession" of Jesus' ancestors and Luke records the physical descent. Furthermore, Matthew's is a mnemonic list, grouping names into blocks of fourteen. Two points are important to understand about these genealogies. First, a standard practice in ancient genealogical records was to skip some generations but still refer to an earlier relative as "the father of" purely on the basis of lineage. Second, the difference between Matthew's genealogy and that of Luke is that Matthew traces Christ's ancestry through King Solomon, while Luke does so through the prophet Nathan. Furthermore, Matthew's clear purpose in writing to a Jewish audience was to establish the legal right for Christ to be the heir to King David's throne. Consequently, the line is only taken back to the patriarch Abraham. Luke, however, seeks to establish Christ's lineage to all human beings as the "Son of Man" and, consequently, extends it back to Adam. Additionally, Matthew's wording indicates that he is establishing Jesus' lineage through Joseph as the legal though not biological father of Jesus. Luke, on the other hand, traces Jesus' actual human lineage through his mother, Mary.[8] Significantly, the issue of Jesus' genealogies has not been regarded by the Christian church as a problem when it has sought throughout its history to explain "difficult" passages of Scripture.

Assertions #2 and #3: *The Gospels in general are not reliable accounts of what happened, and none of the Gospel writers knew Jesus personally, nor are their identities even known.* Early church tradition, which ought to count for something in the history of Christianity, held that the apostles Matthew and John knew Jesus, and that Mark was almost certainly the traveling companion of Peter, who knew Jesus. John, the disciple "whom Jesus loved," obviously knew Jesus. The style and vocabulary used by the writer of the three "epistles" of John in the New Testament match almost perfectly the style of the fourth Gospel, indicating that the same person wrote both the Gospel of John and the epistles of John. One of the most prominent leaders of the early Christian church, Polycarp (AD 69–155), who was martyred for his faith, personally knew the apostle John, and he told one of his followers, the early church writer Irenaeus (who lived in the second century, dates uncertain), that John had written the fourth Gospel.

As for Luke, he was a traveling companion of the apostle Paul and wrote the book of Acts, which recounts the evangelistic efforts of the apostles, most notably Peter and Paul. Almost all biblical scholars agree that the same writer penned both the book of Acts and the Gospel of Luke. Twentieth-century scholarship has confirmed archaeologically almost every single detailed designation of places, names, and titles in the book of Acts. One can therefore logically assume that the same care taken in writing the book of Acts was applied to the Gospel of Luke. Luke, who by tradition was a physician, would have been expected to write good Greek, which he indeed did.

Assertion #4: *The translation of the Hebrew word* almah *as "virgin" is incorrect (as in "a virgin shall be with child").* The word *almah* in biblical Hebrew certainly meant a "young woman," and not specifically a "virgin," as the atheists point out. In the overwhelming majority of usages of *almah* in the Old Testament, however, it clearly designates a woman who has not been married and was, according to the norms of the time, by definition a virgin.

Assertion #5: *Jesus never claimed to be divine.* The Gospel of John offers the clearest affirmation that Jesus wanted his disciples to believe that he was indeed God. In John 1:49, Nathanael exclaims, on meeting Jesus, "Rabbi, you are the Son of God; you are the King of Israel." In John 20:28, when Jesus appears after his resurrection to the apostle Thomas (who was not there the first time Jesus appeared to his disciples), Thomas says, "My Lord and my God!" In John 5:17-18, some Jews are described as plotting to kill Jesus because he had stated that he was God, which was blasphemy according to Jewish law, and therefore punishable by death.

The claims of Jesus to be the Son of God are also very clear in the other three Gospels, the so-called synoptic Gospels (Matthew, Mark, and Luke). At Jesus' trial before the Sanhedrin, he is asked specifically whether he is the Son of God. He responds, "You are right in saying I am" (Luke 22:66-70; the parallel passages in the other Synoptics are Matthew 26:62-65 and Mark 14:61-63). From the immediate reaction of the members of the Sanhedrin ("He has spoken blasphemy! Why do we need any more witnesses?" Matthew 26:65), it is clear that what outraged Jewish legal authorities at the time more than anything else was Jesus' claim to divine status. Throughout the Synoptics, Jesus refers to God as *his* father, not *our* father. In the garden of Gethesame, when Jesus is contemplating his own death by crucifixion, he uses the peculiarly intimate address to God in prayer, *Abba*, which is the Hebrew equivalent of "Daddy." Dawkins's assertion that Jesus never thought of himself as divine is contradicted by many New Testament references that clearly show that the Jewish authorities of the day were satisfied—and outraged—that Jesus had indeed claimed divinity.

Assertion #6: *The Gospels differ in their accounts of the resurrection of Jesus.* The resurrection of Jesus, if it occurred, quite obviously is the central event of all human history. It is extraordinary that the Four Horsemen do not even bother to deal with the issue, since if they could decisively prove that it never took place, the entire Christian component of global theism would collapse like a house of cards.

Needless to say, many people have tried hard to disprove the Resurrection. Interestingly, many of them have ended up accepting that the evidence for this startling event is just too overwhelming to dismiss. (Some of the better books affirming the historicity of the Resurrection are included in the bibliography.) The historical case for the Resurrection has been argued persuasively and in detail by many scholars and theologians. For our purposes here, I'll make just three important initial points.

First, contrary to what Hitchens asserts, remarkable unanimity exists in the Gospels on some features of the Resurrection, features that are so unlikely that they demand a much better explanation than that provided by the Four Horsemen. For instance, all four Gospels agree that women were the first witnesses that the Resurrection had occurred. In today's world, nobody would even spare that a thought, but in first-century Palestine, a woman's word was so utterly without value that testimony from women was not accepted in court. It is entirely counterintuitive, therefore, if one is fabricating a story, to set women as the first eyewitnesses of an event that one wants everyone to believe really occurred.

Second, the tomb of Jesus was empty. Both the followers of Jesus who were convinced that he had been resurrected and their opponents in the Jewish community clearly believed that *something had happened to the body of Jesus.* The Gospel accounts make clear that the disappearance of the body from its known burial place led to accusations that Jesus' followers had stolen the body. The apostle Paul, who was converted a year after the Crucifixion, wrote in his first letter to the Corinthians (1 Corinthians 15:3-5), "For what I received I passed on to you as of first importance: that Christ died for our sins according to the Scriptures, that he was buried, that he was raised on the third day according to the Scriptures, and that he appeared to Peter, and then to the Twelve." This passage has been largely accepted as a very early Christian creed, a formula that Paul probably heard from the very early believers on his first visit to Jerusalem, which took place about three years after his conversion and therefore only about four years after Jesus' crucifixion and resurrection.

It is unlikely that any part of the Resurrection story was the product of legend because legends usually require at least one or two generations to bring to life. None of the apocryphal gospels—that is, the so-called Gospel of Judas or the Gospel of Thomas—appeared in the first century after Christ. This is because the eyewitnesses to the life of Jesus and indeed to the Resurrection were still alive. It was not until the living acquaintances of Jesus had died off that any possible apocryphal legend about his life, death, and resurrection could have come into existence.

Third, the initial growth of Christianity was clearly based on the belief that Jesus had been resurrected. The eleven disciples who remained loyal to Jesus believed that they had seen the resurrected Jesus—and they told everyone else so. The early creed to which Paul referred in 1 Corinthians 15:3-5 goes on in the next verse to say that the resurrected Jesus appeared at one point to no fewer than five hundred people. The early Christians were famous for their willingness to die rather than deny Jesus. Of course, there are believers in many religions who are willing to die for what they believe; Islam is only the most recent dramatic example. But it is exceedingly unlikely that the early Christians would have died for something they *knew* to be a falsehood—that is, the claim that Jesus had indeed risen from the dead. So we are left with the highly improbable notion of the simultaneous collective hallucination of several hundred men and women on several different occasions. To believe that, you would have to be an evolutionary biologist from Oxford University, a philosophy professor at Tufts University, a Buddhist graduate student in California, or an Oxford University ex-Trotskyist (with or without a penchant for the bottle).

# RECOMMENDED READING

Archer, Gleason. *A Survey of Old Testament Introduction.* Chicago: Moody Press, 1964.

———. *New Encyclopedia of Bible Difficulties.* Grand Rapids, MI: Zondervan, 1982.

Blomberg, Craig. *The Historical Reliability of the Gospels.* Downers Grove, IL: InterVarsity Press, 1987. See also works by William Lane Craig.

Bruce, F. F. *The Canon of Scripture.* Downers Grove, IL: InterVarsity Press, 1988.

———. *The New Testament Documents: Are They Reliable?* 6th rev. ed. Grand Rapids, MI: Eerdmans, 1981.

Ewert, David. *A General Introduction to the Bible: From Ancient Tablets to Modern Translations.* Grand Rapids, MI: Zondervan, 1983.

Gaebelein, Frank E., ed. *The Expositor's Bible Commentary.* Vol. 1. London: Pickering and Inglis, 1979.

Greenlee, J. Harold. *Introduction to New Testament Textual Criticism.* Grand Rapids, MI: Eerdmans, reprinted 1989.

Metzger, Bruce. *The Text of the New Testament: Its Transmission, Corruption and Restoration.* 3rd ed. Oxford: Oxford University Press, 1992.

# Endnotes

## CHAPTER ONE : THE FOUR HORSEMEN

1. I fess up to borrowing shamelessly a literary notion from Richard Dawkins, who, on page 99 of *The God Delusion*, refers to three eminent British scientists who are men of religious faith (Peacocke, Stannard, and Polkinghorne) "with the likeable familiarity of senior partners in a firm of Dickensian lawyers."

2. David P. Barash, "The DNA of Religious Faith," *The Chronicle of Higher Education*, 20 April 2007, 6.

3. Mao Tse-tung died in September 1976. On the night of October 6, his wife, Jiang Qing, and three of her Shanghai-based political cohorts were arrested in Beijing in a political coup designed to bring an end to Mao's radical leftist policies.

4. Richard Dawkins, "Observer Diary 27th May 2007." Available online at http://richarddawkins.net/article,1195,Observer-Diary-27th-May-2007,Richard-Dawkins (cited June 2007).

5. The human character in the "Opus" strip comments, "Man, here's a surprising trend: atheist books are suddenly best-sellers!" His friend, the penguin Opus of the comic strip's name, suggests that it's not surprising that people might prefer not to believe in God. After all, Opus says, "I'm not crazy about the idea of the maker of the universe knowing my most private, embarrassing secrets."

6. This comment was made by David Steinberger, CEO of Perseus Books LLC, which has signed Christopher Hitchens on to edit *The Portable Atheist*, a compilation of essays by such writers as Mark Twain and Charles Darwin. As reported by Jeffrey A. Trachtenberg, "Hitchens Book Debunking the Deity Is Surprise Hit," *Wall Street Journal*, 22 June 2007, B1.

7. "The Latest Numbers, Newsweek Poll, 31 March 2007: Conducted by Princeton Survey Research Associates International," *Newsweek*. Available online at http://www.msnbc.msn.com/id/17875540/site/newsweek (cited June 2007).

8. "Atheists identified as America's most distrusted minority, according to new U of M study," UMNnews press release, 28 March 2006. Available online at http://www.ur.umn.edu/FMPro?-db=releases&-lay=web&-format=umnnewsreleases/releasesdetail.html&ID=2816&-Find (cited June 2006).

9. Stephen Phillips, "All Things Bright May Not Be So Beautiful," *The Times Higher Education Supplement*, 12 January 2007.

10. Penny Edgell, Joseph Gerteis, and Douglas Hartmann, "Atheists As 'Other': Moral Boundaries and Cultural Membership in American Society," *American Sociological Review*, vol. 71, no. 2 (April 2006), 211–234.

11. Richard Dawkins, *The God Delusion* (London: Bantam Press, 2006), 4.

12. Ibid., 375–379.

13. Steven Waldman, NPR commentary, 4 September 2003. Available online at http://www.the-brights.net/vision/essays/waldman_futrell_geisert_npr.html (cited September 2007).

14. Christopher Hitchens, *God Is Not Great: How Religion Poisons Everything* (New York: Twelve, 2007), 5.

15. R. J. Eskow, "I have a problem with all fundamentalists, even atheists: The world might be better off without organized religion, but who knows?" *Chicago Sun-Times*, 7 January 2007, B5.

16. Michael Novak, "Remembering the Secular Age," *First Things*, June/July 2007.

17. See in particular Christopher Hitchens's interview on Jon Stewart's *The Daily Show* on April 30, 2007. Available online at: http://www.thedailyshow.com/video/index.jhtml?videoid=85999&title=christopher-hitchens (cited November 2007).

18. A cover story by Gary Wolf in the November 2006 issue of *Wired* magazine, "The Church of the Non-Believers," has this amusing narrative:

> At dinner parties or over drinks, I ask people to declare themselves. "Who here is an atheist?" I ask.
>
> Usually, the first response is silence, accompanied by glances all around in the hope that somebody else will speak first. Then, after a moment, somebody does, almost always a man, almost always with a defiant smile and a tone of enthusiasm. He says happily, "I am!"
>
> But it is the next comment that is telling. Somebody turns to him and says: "You would be."
>
> "Why?"
>
> "Because you enjoy p—ing people off."
>
> "Well, that's true."

Available online at http://www.wired.com/wired/archive/14.11/atheism.html?pg=2&topic=atheism&topic_set= (cited June 2007).

19. See my Global Prognosis column in *Christianity Today*'s August 2007 issue, entitled "Attack Dogs of Christianity."

20. As of June 2007, at least three books had been published in response to the atheist onslaught: Michael Patrick Leahy, *Letter to an Atheist* (Nashville: Harpeth River Press, 2007); Andrew Wilson, *Deluded by Dawkins: A Christian Response to* The God Delusion (Eastbourne: Kingsway Communications Ltd., 2007); and R. C. Metcalf, *Letter to a Christian Nation: Counter Point* (New York: iUniverse, 2007).

21. Sam Harris, *Letter to a Christian Nation* (New York: Alfred A. Knopf, 2006), vii.

22. "Toward a Hidden God," *Time* magazine, 8 April 1966. Available online at http://www.time.com/time/magazine/article/0,9171,835309,00.html (cited July 2007).

23. Harris, *Letter to a Christian Nation*, ix.

24. David Aikman, *A Man of Faith: The Spiritual Journey of George W. Bush* (Nashville: W Publishing, 2004), 3.

25. *Newsweek* Poll, "Religious identification in the U.S.: How American adults view themselves," Ontario Consultants on Religious Tolerance. Available online at http://www.religioustolerance.org/chr_prac2.htm (cited June 2007).

26. "Barna's Annual Tracking Study Shows Americans Stay Spiritually Active, But Biblical Views Wane," The Barna Update, The Barna Group, 21 May 2007. Available online at http://www.barna.org/FlexPage.aspx?Page=Barn aUpdate&BarnaUpdateID=271 (cited June 2007).

27. The First Amendment to the U.S. Constitution reads: "Congress shall make no law respecting an establishment of religion, or prohibiting the free exercise thereof; or abridging freedom of speech, or of the press; or of the right of the people peaceably to assemble, and to petition the Government for a redress of grievances."

28. Details of the Ruse-Dawkins spat come from Madeleine Bunting, "Why the Intelligent Design Lobby thanks God for Richard Dawkins: Anti-religious Darwinists are promulgating a false dichotomy between faith and science that gives succor to creationists," *The Guardian*, 27 March 2006, 27. Available online at http://www.templeton-cambridge.org/fellows/bunting/ publications/2006.03.27/why_the_intelligent_design_lobby_thanks_ god_for_richard_dawkins/ (cited September 2007).

29. Polls in the second half of June 2007 found President Bush's approval rating ranging from 26 percent to 32 percent. From "President Bush—Overall Job Rating in recent national polls," PollingReport.com. Available online at http://www.pollingreport.com/BushJob.htm (cited June 2007).

30. Lynn Andriani, "Believe It or Not," *Publishers Weekly*, 4 June 2007. Available online at http://www.samharris.org/site/full_text/believe-it-or-not/ (cited July 2007).

31. A. N. Wilson, *God's Funeral* (London: Abacus, 2000), 465.

32. See my profile of Aleksandr Solzhenitsyn in *Great Souls: Six Who Changed the Century* (Nashville: Word Publishing, 1998), 125–189.

33. Wilson, *God's Funeral*, 466.

34. What Mark Twain actually said was, "The reports of my death are greatly exaggerated."

## CHAPTER TWO: THE ATTACK OF THE FOUR HORSEMEN

1. Dawkins, *The God Delusion*, 153.

2. Ibid., 117.

3. Ibid., 252.

4. Ibid., 278.

5. Ibid., 292.

6. Daniel Dennett, *Breaking the Spell* (New York: Penguin Group, 2006), 181.

7. Ibid., 323.

8. Ibid., 299.

9. Terry Eagleton, "Lunging, Flailing, Mispunching," *London Review of Books*, vol. 28, no. 20 (19 October 2006). Available online at http://www.lrb.co.uk/v28/n20/eagl01_.html (cited October 2007).

10. Ian Parker, "Richard Dawkins's Evolution: An irascible don becomes a surprising celebrity," *The New Yorker*, 9 September 1996. Available online at http://www.simonyi.ox.ac.uk/dawkins/WorldOfDawkins-archive/Media/dawkny.shtml (cited June 2007).

11. Alessandro Lanni, "Breaking the spell of Religion," Reset Dialogues on Civilizations, 21 May 2007. Available online at http://www.resetdoc.org/EN/Dennett-interview.php (cited June 2007).

12. Daniel Dennett, "The Bright Stuff," *The New York Times*, 12 July 2003.

Available online at http://www.the-brights.net/vision/essays/dennett_nyt_article.html (cited June 2007).

13. Oxford and Cambridge universities used to employ four classes of honors degrees, with a first being approximately equivalent to "cum laude" and a fourth a barely passing grade. Fourths have now been abolished at all British universities, and the second class is divided into two halves, the low half approximating to the old "third." In the interests of full disclosure, the present author has to admit that he himself received a third from Oxford five years before Hitchens.

14. Wikipedia.org lists the following books with Christopher Hitchens as the sole author: *God Is Not Great: How Religion Poisons Everything; Thomas Paine's "Rights of Man": A Biography; Thomas Jefferson: Author of America; Love, Poverty, and War: Journeys and Essays; Why Orwell Matters; The Trial of Henry Kissinger; Letters to a Young Contrarian; Unacknowledged Legislation: Writers in the Public Sphere; No One Left to Lie To: The Triangulations of William Jefferson Clinton* (reissued as *No One Left to Lie To: The Values of the Worst Family* in 2000); *The Missionary Position: Mother Teresa in Theory and Practice; For the Sake of Argument: Essays and Minority Reports; Blood, Class, and Nostalgia: Anglo-American Ironies* (reissued 2004, with a new introduction, as *Blood, Class and Empire: The Enduring Anglo-American Relationship*); *The Monarchy: A Critique of Britain's Favorite Fetish; Prepared for the Worst: Selected Essays and Minority Reports; Imperial Spoils: The Curious Case of the Elgin Marbles; Cyprus, Quartet, 1984* (revised editions as *Hostage to History: Cyprus from the Ottomans to Kissinger*).

15. Trachtenberg, "Hitchens Book Is Surprise Hit."

16. "Is God . . . Great" debate with Christopher Hitchens and Chris Hedges, 24 May 2007, King Middle School, Berkeley, California. A video and photo report with partial transcript is available online at http://www.zombietime.com/hitchens-hedges_debate/ (cited October 2007).

17. Jeffrey A. Trachtenberg, "Book Publisher Tries to Stir Up Emotions to Lift Sales," *The Wall Street Journal*, 28 September 2006, sec. B, col. 4, 2.

18. Blair Golson, "Sam Harris: The Truthdig Interview," *truthdig: drilling beneath the headlines*, 3 April 2006. Available online at http://www.truthdig.com/interview/item/20060403_sam_harris_interview/ (cited July 2007).

19. Daniel Dennett, "Thank Goodness," *Edge: The Third Culture*, 3 November

2006. Available online at http://www.edge.org/3rd_culture/dennett06/dennett06_index.html (cited July 2007).

20. On the CNN news talk show *Paula Zahn Now*, when anchor Kyra Phillips reminded viewers that Christopher Hitchens had accused the just-deceased Rev. Jerry Falwell of being "a horrible little person, a vulgar fraud, and a crook" and said "it's a pity there isn't a hell for him to go to," Hitchens riposted, "Do you want to just spend all your time whimpering about what I have said? Or do you have any comments . . . ?" From transcript of "Imus Fallout Creating Climate of Fear on Talk Radio?; Muslims in America; Falwell's Legacy," *Paula Zahn Now*, CNN, 22 May 2007. Available online at http://transcripts.cnn.com/TRANSCRIPTS/0705/22/pzn.01.html (cited July 2007).

21. "The Great God Debate," *The Hugh Hewitt Show*, 6 June 2007. The full transcript is available at http://hughhewitt.townhall.com/transcripts/Transcript.aspx?ContentGuid=2fbc257d-4761-43ff-adfd-279a3e01f69b.

22. Dawkins, *The God Delusion*, 5.

23. Ibid., 6.

24. Dennett, *Breaking the Spell*, 53.

25. Ibid., 21.

26. Mark Oppenheimer, "Hitchens' Glaring Error," *The Huffington Post*, 2 May 2007. Available online at http://www.huffingtonpost.com/mark-oppenheimer/hitchens-glaring-error_b_47480.html (cited June 2007).

27. Hitchens, *God Is Not Great*, 5.

28. Ibid., 6.

29. Karl Marx, "Introduction," *A Contribution to the Critique of Hegel's Philosophy of Right*, Deutsch-Franzosische Jahrbucher, February 1844. Available online at http://marx.eserver.org/1844-intro.hegel.txt (cited July 2007).

30. Hitchens, *God Is Not Great*, 12.

31. Harris, *Letter to a Christian Nation*, viii–ix.

32. Ibid., 91.

33. Thomas May, "Interview with Sam Harris: The Mortal Dangers of Religious Faith," Amazon.com, no date given. Available online at http://www.amazon.com/gp/feature.html?docId=542154 (cited October 2007).

34. Sam Harris, *The End of Faith* (New York: W. W. Norton and Company 2005), 199.

35. Ibid., 52–53.
36. Harris, *Letter to a Christian Nation*, 23–24.
37. Ibid., 24.

## CHAPTER THREE: THEY DON'T LIKE GOD

1. Cited in obituary of Jean Baudrillard, *The Daily Telegraph*, 8 March 2007. Available online at http://www.telegraph.co.uk/news/main.jhtml?xml=/news/2007/03/08/db0801.xml (cited July 2007).
2. Dawkins, *The God Delusion*, 31.
3. Ibid.
4. Ibid., 36.
5. Ibid., 108.
6. Harris, *The End of Faith*, 173.
7. Dawkins, *The God Delusion*, 37.
8. Dennett, *Breaking the Spell*, 265.
9. Dawkins, *The God Delusion*, 239–247.
10. Ibid., 246.
11. Ibid., 241.
12. Ibid., 247.
13. Ibid., 248.
14. Harris, *Letter to a Christian Nation*, 8–9.
15. Ibid., 10.
16. Ashley S. Johnson, "The Law of Moses," *Condensed Biblical Cyclopedia. Blue Letter Bible*. Available online at http://blueletterbible.org/study/cbc/cbc54.html (cited July 2007).
17. Hitchens, *God Is Not Great*, 102.
18. Ibid.
19. Ibid., 110.
20. Ibid.
21. Harris, *Letter to a Christian Nation*, ix.
22. Hitchens, *God Is Not Great*, 254.
23. Ibid., 203. The citation by Hitchens is credited to Brian Victoria, *Zen at War* (London: Weatherhill, 1997).
24. Christopher Hitchens, *The Missionary Position: Mother Teresa in Theory and Practice* (London: Verso, 1997), passim.
25. Ian Parker, "He knew he was right: How a former socialist became the

Iraq war's fiercest defender," *The New Yorker*, vol. 82, no. 33 (16 October 2006), 150.

26. Dawkins, *The God Delusion*, 292.

27. Harris, *Letter to a Christian Nation*, 35.

28. Hitchens, *God Is Not Great*, 7.

29. Ibid., 7.

30. "The Last Days" page of "Admiral Canaris: The Decent Nazi" on Web site *The Holocaust: Crimes, Heroes and Villains*. Available online at http://www.auschwitz.dk/Canaris/id16.htm (cited September 2007).

31. "Dietrich Bonhoeffer," Online Exhibitions of the United States Holocaust Memorial Museum. Available online at http://www.ushmm.org/museum/exhibit/online/bonhoeffer/b6.htm#21r (cited September 2007).

32. Hitchens, *God Is Not Great*, 241.

33. Cited in Os Guiness, *When No One Sees: The Importance of Character in an Age of Image* (Colorado Springs: NavPress, 2000), 281.

34. Helmuth James von Moltke, *Letters to Freya: A Witness against Hitler* (London: Collins-Harvill, 1991), 408–409. Cited by the Reverend Professor Nigel Biggar in a sermon preached on March 11, 2007, at Christ Church Cathedral Dublin on the centenary of the birth of Helmuth James von Moltke. Available online at http://www.cccdub.ie/dean/sermons/2007/sm070311-biggar.html (cited September 2007).

35. Hitchens, *God Is Not Great*, 173.

36. Ibid., 175.

37. Ibid., 176.

38. The 1964 Nobel Peace Prize presentation speech by Gunnar Jahn, chairman of the Nobel Committee, is available online at http://nobelprize.org/nobel_prizes/peace/laureates/1964/press.html (cited July 2007).

39. Sewell Chan, "Hitchens, Sharpton and Faith," The Empire Zone blog, *The New York Times*, 7 May 2007. Available online at http://empirezone.blogs.nytimes.com/2007/05/07/hitchens-sharpton-and-faith (cited September 2007).

40. Bertrand Russell, *What I Believe* (New York: E. P. Dutton and Co., 1925), 28.

## CHAPTER FOUR: THE SCIENCE PROBLEM

1. Jonathan Miller interviewing Richard Dawkins, "The Atheism Tapes: Jonathan Miller in Conversation," Part 4, BBC Channel Four, aired

9 November 2004. Video available online at http://www.youtube.com/ watch?v=sM3l5WJk6fY; transcript available online at http://tapes.atbhost. com/part4.php (cited July 2007).

2. Hitchens, *God Is Not Great*, 3.

3. Jonathan Miller interviewing Daniel Dennett, "The Atheism Tapes: Jonathan Miller in Conversation," Part 6, BBC Channel Four, 22 November 2004, Video available online at http://www.youtube. com/watch?v=zd6EmF2A3uo; transcript available online at http://tapes. atbhost.com/part6.php.

4. Harris, *The End of Faith*, 215. Harris gets Padmasambhava's dates wrong. He flourished in the mid-eighth century, but Harris says that he was "virtually Muhammed's contemporary." This is factually incorrect. Muhammed died in AD 632 , a full century before the Indian mystic became famous.

5. James Wood, "The Celestial Teapot," *The New Republic*, 18 December 2006, 27. Available online at http://www.tnr.com/doc.mhtml?i=2006121 8&s=wood121806 (cited July 2007).

6. The final chapter of *The Selfish Gene* is available online at http://www. rubinghscience.org/memetics/dawkinsmemes.html (cited September 2007).

7. Biography on Antoine Laurent Lavoisier (1743–1794) Web site. Available at http://www.antoine-lavoisier.com/antoine_lavoiser-biography_006.htm (cited September 2007).

8. Dawkins, *The God Delusion*, 163.

9. Ibid., 165.

10. Ibid.

11. See for example the following studies:
David G. Myers, "On Assessing Prayer, Faith, and Health," *Reformed Review*, vol. 53, no. 2 (2000), 119–126. Available online at http://www. davidmyers.org/Brix?pageID=54 (cited September 2007); and Kathleen M. Clark, Howard S. Friedman, and Leslie R. Martin, "A Longitudinal Study of Religiosity and Mortality Risk, *Journal of Health Psychology*, vol. 4, no. 3, (1999), 381–391, the abstract of which is available online at http:// hpq.sagepub.com/cgi/content/abstract/4/3/381 (cited September 2007). The abstract reads:

> The relation of adult religiosity to longevity was studied in 993 participants from Terman's 70-year Life-Cycle Study. Key social and behavioral variables of physical health, psychological well-being,

socio-economic status, social support, and health behaviors were also considered. Results indicate that women who viewed themselves as more religious in adulthood (approximately age 40) had a lower risk for premature mortality than those who were less religiously inclined. These women had healthier behaviors, more positive feelings about their futures, and reported being somewhat happier than their less religiously inclined peers. In this bright, middle-class, 20th century sample, religiosity among women seems to be part of a generally healthy lifestyle, but not necessarily a direct cause of it.

12. Dawkins, *The God Delusion*, 167–168.

13. Ibid., 204.

14. Dennett, *Breaking the Spell*, 100–101.

15. Stuart Watkins, "The Dangerous Ideas Dennett Won't Touch", *Ready, Steady, Book*, 4 November 2006. Available online at http://www.readysteadybook. com/BookReview.aspx?isbn=0713997893 (cited July 2007).

16. See, for example, *Darwinizing Culture: The Status of Memetics As a Science,* Robert Aunger, ed. (New York: Oxford University Press, 2000), which includes the following essays: "A well-disposed social anthropologist's problems with memes," by Maurice Bloch; "Memes: Universal acid, or a better mouse trap?" by Robert Boyd and Peter J. Richardson; "An objection to the memetic approach to culture," by Dan Sperber; and "If memes are the answer, what is the question?" by Adam Kuper.

17. Dawkins, *The God Delusion*, 191.

18. Ibid., 192.

19. Ibid.

20. Richard Dawkins, *A Devil's Chaplain* (Boston: Houghton Mifflin Company, 2003), 124.

21. Alister McGrath, *Dawkins' God: Genes, Memes, and the Meaning of Life* (Oxford: Blackwell Publishing, 2005), 128.

22. Dawkins, *The God Delusion*, 200–201.

23. McGrath, *Dawkins' God*, 130.

24. Dawkins, *The God Delusion*, 188.

25. Cited in McGrath, *Dawkins' God*, 125.

26. Dennett, *Breaking the Spell*, 14.

27. Ibid., 20.

28. Ibid., 221.

29. Ibid.

30. John Gray, "Atheists are irrational too," *New Statesman*, 20 March 2006. Available online at http://www.newstatesman.com/200603200044 (cited July 2007).

31. Ibid.

32. John Cornwell, "Religion as a Natural Phenomenon," *The Sunday Times*, 19 February 2006. Available online at www.timesonline.co.uk/tol/news/uk/science/article730931.ece (cited July 2007).

33. Leon Wieseltier, "The God Genome" *The New York Times*, 19 February 2006. Available online at http://www.nytimes.com/2006/02/19/books/review/19wieseltier.html?ex=1298005200&en=9ecb4016f9ff8682&ei=5090 (cited September 2007).

34. Stephen Jay Gould, "Impeaching a Self-Appointed Judge," *Scientific American*, vol. 267, no. 1 (1992), 118–121. Available online at http://www.stephenjaygould.org/reviews/gould_darwin-on-trial.html (cited September 2007). Cited in Alister McGrath, *The Dawkins Delusion* (London: Society for Promoting Christian Knowledge, 2007), 13.

35. Dawkins, *The God Delusion*, 57.

36. Ibid., 55.

37. Dawkins, *The God Delusion*, 55, citing Alister McGrath, *Dawkins' God*, 55, who cites Gould, "Impeaching a Self-Appointed Judge."

38. Dawkins, *The God Delusion*, 55–56.

39. Ibid., 56–57.

40. Ibid., 57.

41. Bertrand Russell wrote, "If I were to suggest that between the Earth and Mars there is a china teapot revolving about the sun in an elliptical orbit, nobody would be able to disprove my assertion provided I were careful to add that the teapot is too small to be revealed even by our most powerful telescopes. But if I were to go on to say that, since my assertion cannot be disproved, it is intolerable presumption on the part of human reason to doubt it, I should rightly be thought to be talking nonsense. If, however, the existence of such a teapot were affirmed in ancient books, taught as the sacred truth every Sunday, and instilled into the minds of children at school, hesitation to believe in its existence would become a mark of eccentricity and entitle the doubter to the attentions of the psychiatrist in an enlightened age or of the inquisitor in an earlier time." From "Is

There a God," commissioned by *Illustrated Magazine* but never published, 1952. The full article can be read online at http://www.cfpf.org.uk/articles/religion/br/br_god.html (cited September 2007).

42. Michael Ruse, "Faith and Reason: As the Intelligent Design Case in Dover, Pennsylvania Demonstrates, the Battle Between Science and Religion Rages On," *Playboy*, April 2006, 133.

43. Cited by Dawkins, *The God Delusion*, 67. Dawkins, however, misquotes Jerry Coyne, who wrote a letter to the editor of *Playboy* in response to Ruse's article. Dawkins cites Coyne's response as appearing in the August 2006 issue, but gives no further sourcing information. In fact, Coyne's letter, which was published on p. 15, only has the first part of what Dawkins quotes ("that Ruse 'fails to grasp the real nature of the conflict'") but not the second part (that it is "*real* war . . . between rationalism and superstition").

44. Charles Darwin, *The Autobiography of Charles Darwin, 1809–1882* (London: Collins, 1958), 92–93. Available online at http://darwin-online.org.uk/content/frameset?itemID=F1497&viewtype=text&pageseq=94 (cited September 2007).

45. Ibid., 93.

46. Ibid., 138–139.

47. "Such a Man," *Time*, 31 January 1949. Available online at http://www.time.com/time/magazine/article/0,9171,794511,00.html (cited September 2007).

48. Dawkins, *The God Delusion*, 16.

49. Ibid., 18.

50. Hitchens, *God Is Not Great*, 272.

51. Harris, *The End of Faith*, 271, endnote 44.

52. Walter Isaacson, "Einstein and Faith," *Time*, 5 April 2007. Available online at http://www.time.com/time/magazine/article/0,9171,1607298,00.html (cited July 2007).

53. Ibid.

54. Owen Gingerich, *God's Universe* (Cambridge, MA: Harvard University Press, 2006) and Francis Collins, *The Language of God: A Scientist Presents Evidence for Belief* (New York: The Free Press, 2006).

55. Collins, *The Language of God*, 5–6.

56. Gingerich, *God's Universe*, 101–102.

57. Alfred North Whitehead, *Science and the Modern World* (New York: The Macmillan Company, 1925), 5.

58. Ibid., 16.

59. Ibid., 17–18.

## CHAPTER FIVE: THE PROBLEM OF WICKED ATHEISTS

1. Dawkins, *The God Delusion*, 272.

2. Ibid., 273.

3. Ibid., 274.

4. Adolf Hitler, *Mein Kampf* (New York: Houghton Mifflin, 1969), 60. A 1941 English translation of *Mein Kampf* published by Reynal and Hitchcock is available online at http://ia331334.us.archive.org/2/items/meinkampf035176mbp/meinkampf035176mbp.pdf.

5. Harris, *Letter to a Christian Nation*, 40.

6. Ibid., 41.

7. Roy Hattersley, "Faith does breed charity: We atheists have to accept that most believers are better human beings," *The Guardian*, 12 September 2005. Available online at http://www.guardian.co.uk/comment/story/0,3604,1567604,00.html (cited October 2007).

8. Hitchens, *God Is Not Great*, 230.

9. Ibid., 237.

10. Ibid., 247.

11. Ibid., 248.

12. For an in-depth discussion of the correlation between an emperor's adherence to ancient religious rites and the goodness or wickedness of his rule, see chapter 7 ("God's Country") and chapter 8 ("Enter the Dragon") of *Faith of Our Fathers: God in Ancient China*, by Chan Kei Thong with Charlene L. Fu (Beijing: China Publishing Group Orient Publishing Center, 2006). Distribution of this book, which is available in both English and Chinese, has been limited, but it may be purchased online from http://www.faithofourfathersbooks.com/.

13. See in particular page 226 of Thong and Fu, *Faith of Our Fathers*. It reads in part:

> . . . The allegiance that the people owed the emperor was conditional upon the ruler's ability to have and to hold the Mandate, and the emperor's ability to hold the Mandate was considered conditional

as well. His personal virtues and wisdom in governing determined whether God continued to favor him with the Mandate. If the emperor became immoral or his rule tyrannical, the people would be justified in thinking that he had lost the right to rule and that he and his dynasty should be replaced, even by revolt. . . .

This concept of the Mandate of Heaven gave rise to the cycles of dynastic rule that appeared throughout the millennia of Chinese history: a dynasty over time becomes corrupt and is replaced by a new dynasty that rules with some degree of virtue until it too becomes corrupt, thus repeating the cycle. Of course, not all new rulers were completely virtuous, but the opposite was always true: corrupt emperors did not hold on to the Mandate for long.

14. This doesn't inhibit many atheists—notably Dennett and Harris—from using terms like *moral* and *sacred*, as though the notion of "sacred" had any value at all outside a religious worldview.

15. An interesting discussion of the meaning of this assertion can be found in "If God did not exist, it would be necessary to invent him," *Everything2*. Available online at http://www.everything2.com/index.pl?node_id=776218 (cited August 2007).

16. A. Robert Caponigri, *Philosophy from the Romantic Age to the Age of Positivism* (South Bend, IN: University of Notre Dame Press, 1971), 4.

17. Georg Wihelm Friedrich Hegel, *Early Theological Writings*, trans. T. M. Knox, introduction and fragments translated by Richard Kroner (Chicago: University of Chicago Press, 1948), 6. Available online at http://people. bu.edu/wwildman/WeirdWildWeb/courses/mwt/dictionary/mwt_ themes_460_hegel.htm (cited August 2007).

18. Dawkins, *The God Delusion*, 231.

19. Hitchens, *God Is Not Great*, 10.

20. Ludwig Feuerbach, *The Essence of Christianity*, trans. George Eliot (New York: Harper and Row, 1957), chapter 15. Available online at http://www. marxists.org/reference/archive/feuerbach/works/essence/ec15.htm (cited August 2007).

21. Ibid., 140. Also available online at http://www.marxists.org/reference/ archive/feuerbach/works/essence/ec27.htm (cited August 2007).

22. Karl Marx and Friedrich Engels, *Historische-Kritische Gesamtausgabe*,

11 vols., vol. 1 (Frankfurt-am-Main: Marx-Engels Institut, 1927–1935), 1–2, 261.

23. Cited in Walter Sens, *Karl Marx: Seine irreligiose Entwicklung und anti-Christliche Einstellung* (Halle: Akademischer Verlag, 1935), 38.

24. Karl Marx and Friedrich Engels, *Collected Works*, vol. 1 (London: Lawrence and Wishart, 1975), 30. Also available online at http://www.marxists.org/archive/marx/works/1841/dr-theses/foreword.htm (cited August 2007).

25. Karl Marx, *Early Writings* (Harmondsworth, UK: Penguin Books, 1975), 243–244. Also available online at http://www.marxists.org/archive/marx/works/1843/critique-hpr/intro.htm (cited August 2007).

26. Mikhail Bakunin, *God and the State* (New York: Dover Publications, 1970), 28. Also available online at http://dwardmac.pitzer.edu/Anarchist_Archives/bakunin/godandstate/godandstate_ch1.html#II (cited August 2007).

27. Vladimir Lenin, *Polnoe Sobranie Sochinenii*, 5th ed., vol. 47 (Moscow: Gospolitizdat, 1965–1973), 226–227.

28. M. I. Shakhnovich, *Problemy Ateizma V. I. Lenina* (Leningrad: Izdatel'stvo Akademiee Nauk SSR, 1961), 67.

29. "Religion in the U.S.S.R.: Militant Atheism Becomes a Mass Movement—1934," from *The Communist Conspiracy*, rationalrevolution.net. Available online at http://rationalrevolution.net/special/library/cc835_41.htm (cited September 2007).

30. Aleksandr Solzhenitsyn, *The Gulag Archipelago 1918–1956* (New York: Westview Press, 1991).

31. Ibid., 37–38.

32. Ibid., 37.

33. V. I. Lenin, "Draft Decision for the Politbureau of the C.C. R.C.P.(B.) on the Free Sale of Books from Moscow Warehouse Stocks," in Lenin's *Collected Works*, 1st English ed., vol. 42 (Moscow: Progress Publishers, 1965), 342–343. Available online at http://www.marxists.org/archive/lenin/works/1921/sep/13a.htm (cited October 2007).

34. V. I. Lenin, "Fourth Anniversary of the October Revolution," *Pravda*, no. 234, 18 October 1921, in Lenin's *Collected Works*, 2nd English ed., vol. 33 (Moscow: Progress Publishers, 1965), 51–59. Available online at http://www2.cddc.vt.edu/marxists/archive/lenin/works/1921/oct/14.htm (cited September 2007).

35. Cited in A. A. Valentinov, *The Assault of Heaven* (London: Boswell Printing and Publishing Co., 1925), 9.
36. Cited ibid., 7.
37. V. I. Lenin, *Selected Works in Three Volumes*, vol. 3 (Moscow: Progress Publishers, 1970), 476–477.
38. Symbolically, one of the first major acts of the Yeltsin post-Communist government in the 1990s was to give permission and valuable funding for a complete reconstruction of the cathedral in its original form. This was completed and the cathedral formally consecrated in 2000. It is the largest church in Russia today. During its construction, an exhibit next to the site showed videotapes of the dynamiting that Stalin ordered of the original cathedral.
39. Donald W. Treadgold, *Twentieth Century Russia*, 2nd ed. (Chicago: Rand McNally and Company, 1959), 351.
40. For a detailed study of the history of Christianity in China, including Communist persecution of the church from 1949 to today, see the updated version of my book *Jesus in Beijing: How Christianity Is Transforming China and Changing the Global Balance of Power* (Washington, DC: Regnery Publishing, 2006).
41. *Jesus in Beijing*, 68.
42. Jung Chang and Jon Halliday, *Mao: The Unknown Story* (London: Jonathan Cape, 2005), 13.
43. Stéphane Courtois and others, *The Black Book of Communism: Crimes, Terror, Repression* (Cambridge, MA: Harvard University Press, 1999), xiv–xv.
44. Ibid., 616.
45. Y Phandara, *Retour à Phnom Penh: le Cambodge du génocide à la colonization* (Paris: A.M. Métailié, 1982), 88, cited in Courtois et al., *The Black Book of Communism,* 616.
46. *Phnom Penh Post*, 20 September 1996, 7, cited in Courtois et al *The Black Book of Communism*, 630.
47. Tzvetan Todorov, *On Human Diversity* (Cambridge, MA: Harvard University Press, 1993), 170.
48. Courtois et al., *The Black Book of Communism,* 755.
49. Ibid.
50. Friedrich Nietzsche, *The Joyful Wisdom*, Sections 125 and 343, in William

V. Spamos, *A Casebook on Existentialism* (New York: Crowell, 1966), cited in Os Guinness, *The Journey* (Colorado Springs, CO: NavPress, 2001), 137–138.

51. Adolf Hitler, *Table Talk*, cited in Alan Bullock, *Hitler: A Study in Tyranny* (New York: Konecky and Konecky, 1962), 672–673.

52. Richard Grunberger, *A Social History of the Third Reich* (London: Phoenix, 2005), cited in Edward Bartlett-Jones, "Hitler and Christianity," Bede's Library. Available online at http://www.bede.org.uk/hitler.htm (cited August 2007).

53. Harris, *Letter to a Christian Nation*, 23–24.

## CHAPTER SIX: THE CHRISTIAN WORLDVIEW IS THE FOUNDATION OF LIBERTY

1. Michael Novak, speech to Library of Congress, 1998. Cited in Os Guinness, *The Great Experiment* (Colorado Springs: Navpress, 2001), 136.

2. Dawkins, *The God Delusion*, 39.

3. Hitchens, *God Is Not Great*, 66.

4. "The Mayflower Compact (1620)," *Basic Readings in U.S. Democracy*, U.S. Information Agency. Available online at http://usinfo.state.gov/usa/infousa/facts/democrac/2.htm (cited October 2007).

5. Dawkins, *The God Delusion*, 40.

6. Ibid.

7. William Wilberforce was only twenty-five when he experienced his conversion in 1785, but he had by then already been a member of parliament for four years. Within two years of his conversion, he recognized his life's calling. Writing in his diary on October 28, 1787, he recorded these famous words: "God Almighty has set before me two great objects, the suppression of the Slave Trade and the Reformation of Manners," by which he meant, in modern terms, "habits, attitudes, and morals." From John Pollock, "William Wilberforce: A Man Who Changed His Times," The Trinity Forum Reading series, 1996 and 2003, 13–15.

8. Michael Novak, *On Two Wings: Humble Faith and Common Sense at the American Founding* (San Francisco: Encounter Books, 2002), 129.

9. Thomas Paine, *The Age of Reason* (New York: Citadel Press, 1974), 50. Available online at http://www.atheistsunited.org/wordsofwisdom/Edwards/paine.html (cited August 2007).

10. Thomas Paine, "The Existence of God: A Discourse at The Society of

Theophilanthropists, Paris." Available online at http://www.infidels.org/library/historical/thomas_paine/existence_of_god.html (cited August 2007).

11. Christopher Hitchens, *Thomas Jefferson: Author of America* (New York: HarperCollins, 2005).

12. Thomas Jefferson, Letter to Peter Carr, 1787, *The Writings of Thomas Jefferson*, Memorial Edition, vol. 6 (Washington, DC: Jefferson Memorial Association, 1903–1904), 258. Also available online at http://etext.virginia.edu/jefferson/quotations/jeff0700.htm (cited October 2007).

13. Thomas Jefferson, "Letters: The Morals of Jesus, to Dr. Benjamin Rush, with a Syllabus," April 21, 1803. Available online at http://www.positiveatheism.org/hist/jeff1122.htm (cited August 2007).

14. Thomas Jefferson, "Notes on the State of Virginia," 1782, from "Quotations on the Jefferson Memorial," *Thomas Jefferson's Monticello* Web site. Available online at http://www.monticello.org/reports/quotes/memorial.html.

15. This incident is recounted by Ethan Allen in a brief history called "Washington Parish, Washington City" that he wrote in approximately 1857. The original manuscript, a small, string-bound edition without pagination, is kept at shelf location MMC-1167 in the Manuscript Division of the Library of Congress. The Jefferson story is located toward the end of the booklet. (Many thanks to Manuscript Reference Librarian Bruce Kirby of the Library of Congress for this information.) The *Thomas Jefferson's Monticello* Web site's Jefferson Library, however, is skeptical about the authenticity of this incident. See http://www.monticello.org/library/reference/spurious.html (cited August 2007).

16. Benjamin Franklin, "Constitutional Convention Address on Prayer," delivered June 28, 1787. Available online at http://www.americanrhetoric.com/speeches/benfranklin.htm.

17. Lester J. Cappon, ed., *The Adams-Jefferson Letters: The Complete Correspondence between Thomas Jefferson and Abigail and John Adams* (Chapel Hill, NC: The University of North Carolina Press, 1959), 509.

18. Ibid., 513.

19. In *On Two Wings*, p. 34, Michael Novak frames the issues thus:
    Liberty is the object of the Republic.
    Liberty needs virtue.
    Virtue among the people is impossible without religion.

20. Benjamin Rush, "Of the Mode of Education Proper in a Republic, 1798," *Selected Writings,* 87–89, 92, 94–96, from *The Founders' Constitution,* Philip B. Kurland and Ralph Lerner, eds., vol. 1 (Chicago: The University of Chicago Press, 2000), chapter 18, document 30. Available online at http://press-pubs.uchicago.edu/founders/documents/v1ch18s30.html.

21. Ibid.

22. Ibid.

23. Charles Francis Adams, ed., *The Works of John Adams, Second President of the United States,* vol. 2 (Boston: Little, Brown, and Company, 1850–1856), 356.

24. "In the Liberal Tradition: John Witherspoon," *Religion and Liberty,* vol. 7, no. 5 (September and October 1997). Also available online at http://www.acton.org/publicat/randl/liberal.php?id=249 (cited August 2007).

25. James Madison, "Speech in the Virginia Ratifying Convention on the Judicial Power," June 20, 1788. Available online at http://www.constitution.org/rc/rat_va_17.htm (cited August 2007).

26. H. W. Brands, *The First American: The Life and Times of Benjamin Franklin* (Garden City, NJ: Anchor, 2002), 667.

27. Cited in *America's God and Country: Encyclopedia of Quotations,* William J. Federer, ed. (St. Louis: Amerisearch Inc., 2000), 10–11.

28. John Adams, "Letter to Zabdiel Adams, June 21, 1776." Available online at http://www.founding.com/founders_library/pageID.2144/default.asp

29. Harris, *Letter to a Christian Nation,* 24.

30. Hitchens, *God Is Not Great,* 283.

31. Christopher Hitchens, "An Atheist Replies," *The Washington Post,* 14 July 2007, A17. Also available online at http://www.washingtonpost.com/wp-dyn/content/article/2007/07/13/AR2007071301461.html (cited August 2007).

32. Zoltan Haraszti, "John Adams Flays a Philosophe: Annotations on Condorcet's Progress of the Human Mind," *The William and Mary Quarterly,* 3rd ser., vol. 7, no. 2 (April 1950), 223–254. Also available online at http://links.jstor.org/sici?sici=0043-5597%28195004%293%3A7%3A2%3C223%3AJAFAPA%3E2.0.CO%3B2-P (cited August 2007). The article reproduces all of Adams's comments in the text of Condorcet's book. This particular quote is found on page 244 of the book.

33. Ibid. This quote is found on page 241.

34. George Washington, "General Orders on Profanity," 3 August 1776, *The Papers of George Washington* Web site, Alderman Library, University of Virginia. Available online at http://gwpapers.virginia.edu/documents/revolution/profanity_1.html (cited August 2007).

35. George Washington, "The Thanksgiving Proclamation," New York, 3 October 1789, *The Papers of George Washington* Web site, Alderman Library, University of Virginia. Available online at http://gwpapers.virginia.edu/documents/thanksgiving/transcript.html (cited August 2007).

36. George Washington, "The Final Address: Transcript of the Final Manuscript," 19 September 1796, *The Papers of George Washington* Web site, Alderman Library, University of Virginia. Available online at http://gwpapers.virginia.edu/documents/farewell/transcript.html (cited August 2007).

37. "Treaty of Peace and Friendship between the United States and the Bey and Subjects of Tripoli of Barbary," signed and sealed at Algiers, 3 January 1797. Available online at http://www.stephenjaygould.org/ctrl/treaty_tripoli.html and at http://en.wikipedia.org/wiki/Treaty_of_Tripoli#Article_11 (cited August 2007).

38. Alexis de Tocqueville, "Chapter XVII: Principal Causes Maintaining The Democratic Republic—Part III," *Democracy in America*, bk. 1. Available online at http://www.classicallibrary.org/tocqueville/democracy1/34.htm (cited August 2007).

39. Ibid—Part II, *Democracy in America*, bk 1. Available online at http://www.classicallibrary.org/tocqueville/democracy1/33.htm (cited August 2007).

40. Ibid.

41. Ibid.

42. Hitchens, *God Is Not Great*, 179.

43. Cited in Federer, *America's God and Country*, 382.

44. Abraham Lincoln, "Proclamation Appointing a National Fast Day," 30 March 1863. Available online at http://showcase.netins.net/web/creative/lincoln/speeches/fast.htm (cited August 2007).

45. Abraham Lincoln, "To the Synod of the Old School Presbyterians of Baltimore," from *The Lincoln Memorial: Album-Immortelles*, collected and edited by Osborn H. Oldroyd, (New York: G. W. Carleton and Co., Publishers, 1883), 254. Available online at http://varuna.grainger.uiuc.edu/

oca/lincoln/lincolnmemoriala00oldrrich/lincolnmemoriala00oldrrich_
djvu.txt (cited August 2007).

46. George W. Bush, "Remarks at National Hispanic Prayer Breakfast,"
18 May 2002. Available online at http://www.whitehouse.gov/news/
releases/2002/05/20020516-1.html (cited August 2007).

47. The U.S.–based Pew Charitable Trust has funded several programs to
educate journalists in religious matters.

48. See my book *Jesus in Beijing* for the lower estimate. The 13 percent figure
is based on reports of confidential speeches by various Chinese government
figures connected with religious affairs.

49. Aikman, *Jesus in Beijing*, 5.

50. Hong Xu, "God and the Essence of Liberty: A Preliminary Inquiry into the
History of Freedom," paper presented at the 23rd International Meeting of
the Eric Voegelin Society/American Political Science Association, Chicago,
Illinois, 1 September 2007.

51. Yonghai Xu, "Dangjin Shijie Zui Xuyao de shi Shangdi," 30 July 2007.
Privately distributed and made available by Charlene L. Fu.

52. Songmin Guo, "'Lin Daiyu Chujia' de Biaoben Yiyi," *Beijing Wanbao*,
27 February 2007. Available online at http://beijing.qianlong.com/3825/
2007/02/28/3022@3693978.htm (cited August 2007).

## CONCLUSION: THE NEW ATHEISM OFFERS NOTHING NEW

1. David van Biema, "God vs. Science," *Time*, 5 November 2006. Available
online at http://www.time.com/time/magazine/article/0,9171,1555132,00.
html (cited September 2007).

2. Voltaire in a letter to Frederick the Great. Cited by "Quotes: Christianity,"
*Atheism: The Capital Man* Web site. Available online at http://atheisme.
free.fr/Quotes/Christianity.htm (cited November 2007).

3. Lona Manning, "The Murder of Madalyn Murray O'Hair: America's Most
Hated Woman," *Crime*, 29 September 2003. Available online at http://
crimemagazine.com/ohair.htm (cited September 2007).

4. "William J. Murray," Previous Events of the Ezekiel Forum, Central
Pennsylvania Christian Institute, Inc. Available online at http://www.cpci.
org/ezekiel/2002/WilliamJMurray/WilliamJMurray.htm (cited October
2007).

5. Lawrence Wright, *Saints and Sinners* (New York: Alfred A. Knopf,

1993), 114. Also available online at http://www.geocities.com/Athens/Forum/8666/ht-whospeaks.html (cited September 2007).

6. The full text of *Dialogue between a Priest and a Dying Man* is available online at http://www.horrormasters.com/Text/a0293.pdf (cited September 2007).

7. The full text of *Philosophy in the Bedroom* is available online at http://www.sin.org/tales/Marquis_de_Sade--Philosophy_in_the_Bedroom.pdf (cited September 2007).

8. Alister McGrath, *The Twilight of Atheism: The Rise and Fall of Disbelief in the Modern World* (New York: Doubleday, 2004), 34–35 passim.

9. Aldous Huxley, "Confessions of a Professed Atheist," *Report: Perspective on the News*, vol. 3 (June 1966), 19. Cited in Bert Thompson, *Christianity and Humanism*, (Montgomery, AL: Apologetics Press Inc., n.d.), 2. Available online at http://www.apologeticspress.org/rr/reprints/Christianity-and-Humanism.pdf (cited October 2007).

10. McGrath, *The Twilight of Atheism*, 262.

11. The problem was not limited to sociology, psychology, or child rearing, either. When I wrote an essay for *Time* magazine in September 1978 on the genocide in Cambodia, there was intensive discussion among the editors whether what had happened could be described as "evil." Some of the follow-up letters to the editor subsequently complained that they thought it incomprehensible that the weekly newsmagazine had employed "value judgments" to describe what had occurred in what became known as "the killing fields" of Cambodia.

12. Van Biema, "God vs. Science."

13. Harris, *The End of Faith*, 205.

14. Cited in David Aikman, *Billy Graham: His Life and Influence* (Nashville: Thomas Nelson, 2007), 11.

15. Christopher Dawson, *Religion and the Rise of Western Culture* (New York: Doubleday, 1991), 15–16 passim.

16. Rodney Stark, *The Victory of Reason: How Christianity Led to Freedom, Capitalism, and Western Success* (New York: Random House, 2005), xi.

17. Ibid., 11–12.

18. Ibid., 233–235 *passim*.

19. Francis Collins, *The Language of God: A Scientist Presents Evidence for Belief* (New York: Free Press, 2006), 6.

20. See Frank J. Tipler, *The Physics of Christianity* (New York: Doubleday, 2007), 118.
21. Ibid., 124–125.
22. Gould, "Impeaching a Self-Appointed Judge."
23. John Polkinghorne, "Understanding the Universe," *Cosmic Questions, Annals of the New York Academy of Sciences*, vol. 950, December 2001, 175–182. Available online for $15 at: http://www.annalsnyas.org/cgi/content/full/950/1/175 (cited September 2007).

## APPENDIX

1. Hitchens, *God Is Not Great*, 99.
2. Classical scholars do not agree on whether the Carthaginians practiced child sacrifice. See "Child Sacrifice?" *A Bequest Unearthed, Phoenicia, Encyclopedia Phoeniciana*, available online at http://phoenicia.org/childsacrifice.html (cited October 2007).
3. Jeremiah 7:30-31: "'The people of Judah have done evil in my eyes, declares the LORD. They have set up their detestable idols in the house that bears my Name and have defiled it. They have built the high places of Topheth in the Valley of Ben Hinnom to burn their sons and daughters in the fire—something I did not command, nor did it enter my mind."
4. S. Robert Lichter and Stanley Rothman, "Media and Business Elites," *Public Opinion*, October/November 1981. The views on adultery and other findings of the 1981 poll are available online at http://www.mediaresearch.org/biasbasics/biasbasics.asp (cited October 2007).
5. Telephone conversation with the author on August 23, 2007.
6. Dawkins, *The God Delusion*, 97.
7. F. F. Bruce, *The New Testament Documents: Are They Reliable?* (Downers Grove, IL: InterVarsity Press, 1977), 19–20.
8. I am indebted to Dr. Darrel Cox, associate professor of biblical studies at Patrick Henry College. For further information about the genealogies, see Gleason Archer, *The Encyclopedia of Bible Difficulties* (Grand Rapids, MI: Zondervan, 1982).

# ACKNOWLEDGMENTS

Many people have, directly or indirectly, helped me with the writing of this book. Since I myself was once not just an atheist but a militant atheist, I wish to begin by publicly thanking the man who led me out of that morass into a living faith, and who has since gone on to his eternal reward: the late Canon Keith de Berry, rector of St. Aldate's Church, Oxford.

I would like to thank my agent, John Eames, for encouraging me to come up with the proposal for this book, and for gaining the interest of Tyndale House Publishers. At that wonderful publishing house, I am especially grateful to associate publisher Jan Long Harris, who caught the vision for this book from the beginning and encouraged the writing and editing through to completion. Author relations manager Sharon Leavitt eased the process of a visit to Tyndale in Carol Stream, Illinois, and a fruitful planning meeting with many of the company's key officers. Senior editor Lisa A. Jackson presided with patience, steadiness, and expertise over an editing process that was more demanding than usual.

My niece in Cambridge, UK, Fiona Saunderson, kindly let me stay at the home of her and her husband, David, and hosted an excellent dinner where I met some of Cambridge's outstanding scientists who are Christians: Professor John Polkinghorne; Sir Brian Heap, formerly Master of St. Edmunds College, Cambridge, and a founding member of the International Society of Science and Religion; and Chris Coxworth, principal of Ridley Hall, Cambridge.

Dan Russ, senior fellow at the Trinity Forum and director of the Center for Christian Studies at Gordon College, helped with suggestions on handling the appendix and put me in touch with other scholars who were very insightful on matters relating to biblical textual criticism. I am grateful to him as well as to Dr. Rob Wall, P. T. Walls Professor of Scripture at Seattle Pacific University, and Dr. Steve Hunt, associate professor of biblical studies at Gordon College.

My editorial colleague at the Salem Radio Network, talk-show host Hugh Hewitt, offered useful pointers to people who had effectively debated with some of the atheist figures in this book.

Another Salem talk-show host, Dennis Prager, was generous in his analysis of the unique contributions of Judaism to the world of ethics and morality.

Jeannie Light, of Louisa, Virginia, provided useful material and much faithful prayer support.

Last, and in this case most, I want to express a special thanks to my indefatigable editor for several books in a row, Charlene L. Fu, of Beijing, China. In the case of this book, Charlene's initial research, follow-up research, double-checking of sometimes dubious "facts" from the Internet, and concise and meticulous editing were totally indispensable. I owe her gratitude too for putting up with my complaints over her very meticulous editing process. Not many editors can double-check footnotes in German, French, Russian, and Chinese, or provide and translate key Chinese-language material.

Virginia, USA
October 2007

# INDEX

# ABOUT THE AUTHOR

DAVID AIKMAN is a twenty-three year veteran of *Time* magazine, covering headline events around the globe and meeting the leading newsmakers of our times. He is the author of eight books, most notably a groundbreaking account of the church in China and its future worldwide impact, a best-selling biography of President George W. Bush's spiritual life, and an analytical biography of the life and influence of Billy Graham. His forthcoming books include a new novel in the Richard Ireton series and a book about the Middle East.

Dr. Aikman is a columnist on world affairs for *Christianity Today* and writes for news publications including the *Wall Street Journal, The American Spectator,* and *The Weekly Standard.* With special expertise in China, Russia, the Middle East, Mongolia, and religious freedom issues worldwide, he is often asked to provide expert testimony at congressional hearings and to give television commentary in connection with breaking news events. His radio commentaries can be heard regularly on the Salem Communications network. Dr. Aikman also teaches history and writing at Patrick Henry College in Virginia.

# OTHER BOOKS BY DAVID AIKMAN

*Billy Graham: His Life and Influence*
(Thomas Nelson, 2007)

*QI,* novel
(Broadman and Holman Publishers, 2005)

*Man of Faith: The Spiritual Journey of George W. Bush*
(W Publishing Group, 2004)

*Jesus in Beijing: How Christianity Is Transforming China
and Changing the Global Balance of Power*
(Regnery Publishing Inc., 2003; updated paperback, 2006)

*Great Souls: Six Who Changed the Century*
(Word Publishing, 1998; paperback, Lexington Books, 2002)

*Hope: The Heart's Great Quest*
(Servant Publications, 1995)

*When The Almond Tree Blossoms,* novel
(Word Publishing, 1993)

*Pacific Rim: Area of Change, Area of Opportunity*
(Little, Brown and Company, 1986)

ALSO COAUTHOR OF

*Massacre in Beijing: China's Struggle for Democracy*
(Warner Books, 1989)

*Gorbachev: An Intimate Biography*
(New American Library, 1988)

*Love China Today*
(Tyndale House, 1978)

See www.davidaikman.com for announcements of forthcoming books